Tails *From A* Different Perspective

Cindy Downing

BALBOA.
PRESS

A DIVISION OF HAY HOUSE

Balboa Press books may be ordered through booksellers or by contacting:

Balboa Press
A Division of Hay House
1663 Liberty Drive
Bloomington, IN 47403
www.balboapress.com
1 (877) 407-4847

Because of the dynamic nature of the Internet, any web addresses or links contained in this book may have changed since publication and may no longer be valid. The views expressed in this work are solely those of the author and do not necessarily reflect the views of the publisher, and the publisher hereby disclaims any responsibility for them.

The author of this book does not dispense medical advice or prescribe the use of any technique as a form of treatment for physical, emotional, or medical problems without the advice of a physician, either directly or indirectly. The intent of the author is only to offer information of a general nature to help you in your quest for emotional and spiritual well-being. In the event you use any of the information in this book for yourself, which is your constitutional right, the author and the publisher assume no responsibility for your actions.

Print information available on the last page.

ISBN: 978-1-9822-3301-3 (sc)
ISBN: 978-1-9822-3303-7 (hc)
ISBN: 978-1-9822-3302-0 (e)

Library of Congress Control Number: 2019912181

Balboa Press rev. date: 11/12/2019

Contents

Dedication

To the animals, both alive and deceased, who shared their stories with me and encouraged me to share them with the world: I am forever grateful.

Introduction

The 5 W's

Who.

Who am I? My name is Cindy Downing and I am just a normal person living a normal life. I'm also an animal communicator, which is NOT considered "normal" to most people.

I grew up with three other siblings and we were raised Catholic. When I was younger, I played with my invisible friends and my animal friends. My mom was fine with it until I started school and insisted, I needed to start making friends with "real kids." Being an obedient kid, I listened to my mom and stopped chatting with my invisible friends and animal friends, finding a place instead with real kids.

In 1999, I was diagnosed with breast cancer and started praying a lot. I waited for a sign I would survive and continue to thrive in my life. I asked for a yellow bird as a sign to let me know I was going to be okay. One day, I looked out the window and started bawling my eyes out as the sign I had prayed for appeared: a bright yellow finch at the bird feeder. I heard a voice in my head saying, "You are going to be fine and you will be working with us again."

I couldn't believe what I was hearing. First, I was full of joy at the thought of surviving such a deadly disease, and then I was trying to figure out what the words "working with us again" meant exactly. Later I came to realize it meant I would be opening my line of communication with the animal world once again.

I am a cancer survivor. I am an animal communicator. I am a child of God. I am a positive influence on the world.

Why.

Why am I writing this book? I am writing this book because animals have communicated to me on numerous occasions that they want their stories shared with humans. This book is for the animals, both alive and deceased, who have been urging me to get their words onto paper for the world to read.

I hope, after reading this book you, the reader, will be more open to the possibility of animal communication. I hope to create conversations between humans and animals, strengthening the bond between both groups. Without animals, I do not believe humans could continue to exist on this planet. There is so much more to this Earth we call home, and we humans should be more open to things we may not be able to touch or see with our own eyes or ears.

What.

What is this book about? These stories contain animal thoughts, feelings, and views they want humans to know.

In this book, I refer to an animal's caregiver or "owner" as the animal's "human." Animals have told me they do not care for the human's dominant vs. submissive way of thinking. The animals want to have strong relationships with people in more of a give and take relationship. Animals are about joy, fun and laughter. It is much more difficult to have those things in their lives when the human is the dominant figure all the time.

Where.

Where does this information come from? The information in this book comes from my own experiences with animals in sessions and when I am just out and about in nature. Animals are constantly communicating with one another just like humans.

When.

When do the fun animal stories begin? In Chapter 3! I hope you enjoy reading this book and I hope it opens your mind to the possibility. According to animals, life should be fun and full of laughter, and I hope these stories will bring my readers both of these things!

The following pages are things animals have shared with me during sessions. For privacy, I have altered the names of each animal. (Yes, animals want to have their privacy, too!) The animals want you to look at things from a different perspective and realize that they do have intelligence and feelings and are able to communicate with humans. I hope, when you are done reading these stories, you are able to look at animals with a different perspective and have a whole new wonderful relationship with them.

Now let's get started with the amazing things animals have shared with me.

Chapter 1: Death and Dying

Let's cut to the chase and get the heavy stuff out of the way first. Animals have a different view on dying and on death than humans. They don't see it as an end, but as a new beginning. Animals both alive and deceased who have been telling me to write this book have also told me they want to address the topic of death at the start of this book because it's considered so taboo in our culture and can come so much more quickly and unexpectedly to our animal companions. But to them, death is inevitable and not something to fear.

I once had a deceased horse tell me: "You humans get all emotional over death. It is not an ending; it is a new beginning. It's like a new birthday for us when we leave our bodies." This was amazing to hear! I got chills all over my body and my hair stood straight up when the horse spoke to me and, as I am writing this right now, I am getting the same sensation. (When I get chills and my hair stands on end, it's my signal that either what I am saying or what the animal's human is saying is exactly what the animal wants to be communicated and is absolutely true. Keep this in mind while reading!)

Animals do not just disappear forever once they leave their physical bodies, they are still very much alive all around us. They are in a spiritual form most people don't see with their eyes, but the animals are still able to communicate with us from this plane. They send us all kinds of signs to let us know they are around just like our human loved ones who have passed. We just need to be open to the signs. Some signs animals have sent to their humans include "Pennies from Heaven," assorted coins for their jokester humans. Feathers, butterflies, birds, and songs on the radio are other examples.

I once had a dog communicate to me that he was going to send dollar bills to his human. I thought this was really strange because I had only heard of coins being sent. It turned out the human was always telling the dog: "You need to get a job so you can start paying for all of this stuff." So, this sentiment really had meaning: the dog had understood what he had been told here on earth and wanted to make sure his human knew.

When animals send a sign like a butterfly or a bird, it doesn't have to be a real live butterfly or bird. The sign might appear as a picture of a bird or butterfly in a magazine, on a T-shirt, on a birthday card, something you see in a video, or even something on the shelves in a store. Also, if you acknowledge the sign you receive from your deceased animal, you will start receiving additional signs because they are pleased to have reached you.

When I receive feathers from my animals in spirit I acknowledge the feathers by saying out loud, "Thanks, guys, for the feather I just received. I know you're nearby." They love being acknowledged and continue to send me more signs because it makes me happy, and the animals are all about being happy. Later in this book, you will read some amazing stories about the wonderful ways animals have sent signs to their humans.

Sometimes animals who are in the process of dying may need human assistance to cross the "rainbow bridge." Animals have communicated to me that they would like to keep their dignity in their final days instead of being kept alive unnecessarily for human comfort. One dog communicated to me that he did *not* want his human to put a diaper on him because it would take away his dignity. When that day came, the dog would be ready to leave his physical body.

Animals do not like the terminology "euthanize" or being "put down." They have told me again and again: they do not want humans to have such a negative attitude toward death. I have been told by several animals that they would like to "be released of their energy here on earth and expand to their new place." (Doesn't that sound so much better than being "put down?")

I have been part of an animal grief support group and the animals have told me they do not want their human to have any guilt for the decision of "releasing them to the other side." Animals don't want to see their humans mourning when they are on earth, and they certainly don't want their humans to mourn when they are no longer in their animal body form. Our animals have not truly left us; they are still nearby in spirit form. They want us to stop worrying about whether we have done the right thing in releasing them, or whether we should have done it sooner, or if we could have saved them in some way. Most animals know that they are here for a short amount of time compared to humans, and they want to make the best of their time with us.

My dog Darcy had a very close bond with another dog, and I was very blessed to be able to communicate with him before he crossed over the rainbow bridge. He expressed loving messages to his humans and told them what signs to look for that his presence was near. "This is not goodbye," he said. "I'll see you later!"

When I got home, I sat down and told Darcy the news. I was crying when I told her. Darcy's response was: "Why are you crying and so sad? You know how this works? He is only gone in body. I can still play and communicate with him. You can still communicate with him. He has just moved to a different form. He is still very much alive, and you know that because of the work you do."

This was such an "Aha!" moment for me. Here I was getting all emotional, and she comforted me, reminding me what the cycle of life is really about. We may be gone in body, but we are still close to our loved ones in spirit. Even though I am an animal communicator, I still don't understand all the mysteries of life and death. This discussion with Darcy was quite enlightening.

Do animals cross the "rainbow bridge?" Do they go to heaven or some other afterlife? It depends on the animal and their human's belief system. In sessions when I have communicated with a deceased animal, they will show me a rainbow bridge to give their human comfort and to validate that it does exist. I have also been shown the words "heaven" and lots of bright lights from animals that have crossed over because that might be what is most important to their human. Animals want to communicate that they are safe and at peace to give their humans comfort and healing.

Chapter 2: Frequently Asked Questions

Over the years, I have encountered some questions that are asked frequently and wanted to share them with you.

How important is an animal's name?

The name of an animal is undeniably very important to them. It is their first impression when they are introduced to humans and other animals. If an animal has a respectable name, it gains more respect from both animals and humans. If they are called something goofy or degrading, this will define them for their entire lives. So, choose your animal's name wisely.

Once, I visited a horse stable and the two women I was with asked me to see if a particular horse liked his name. They did not tell me his name, but they were laughing and joking under their breath when I turned to ask the horse.

"This is bullshit," said the horse.

I couldn't believe what I was hearing and asked him to repeat himself. Again, the same words were said to me. I turned to the women, shook my head, and said, "I don't understand why he is telling me this, but he says, 'This is bullshit.'"

The two women about fell over from laughter.

Finally, one of them said, "His name is Crappy."

Well, no wonder he was unhappy with his name! I asked him if he would like a new name and he communicated that he would like to be called George or Cash (like Johnny Cash) because he was a black horse.

I informed the women that he indeed wanted a new name, and they said they would pass along these ideas to the horse's human. I don't know if the horse got a new name, but I can assure you that I will always remember him!

How can I help my rescue
animal settle in better?

When you adopt an animal from either a rescue shelter or another home, there are a few things I recommend to ease the adjustment. First, take time every day for 2 or 3 weeks to tell the animal out loud that this is his or her "forever home." Let your animal know you are *so* happy they have joined the family and, wherever you may relocate, they will be relocating with you. This is so important to the animals.

I can't tell you how many animals I have communicated with who tell me they don't know whether they are coming or going. When you become frustrated with an animal who has done something incorrect like peeing on the floor or tearing up furniture, please take a few deep breaths before speaking out loud to the animal. I have had animals communicate to me that their humans have said, "If you don't stop peeing on the floor, you are going to find a new home." The human didn't really mean the animal would be going to a new home, but the animal takes it literally. Some animals have communicated that their humans have told them so many times they are going to find a new home, they continue to do the bad behavior because it will get them to their new home even quicker.

Second, take time each day to spend quiet time with the animal and tell them what sort of things you envision doing together in the future, such as walking or hiking trails, running around at the park, being a therapy dog, or just being a best friend and companion. Animals like to have a "job" or a purpose. Just like humans like to have a purpose, animals also need to feel like they have accomplished something each day.

Do animals really understand what humans say?

Yes, animals absolutely understand what humans are saying. Some scientists say that animals do not have brains like humans and that animals could not possibly understand what we are talking about. However, in my experiences with the animals and the numerous sessions I have had with them, they tell me things that would be impossible to explain if they didn't understand our language. If they didn't understand what humans were saying, how could they possibly know some of the things they know?

Once a cat communicated to me that her human was going to Florida in 2 weeks and that the neighbor would be taking care of her. How would she know this and be able to communicate it to me if she didn't understand her human? Answer: she wouldn't!

While animals understand what we say, this does not translate into complete obedience. They have minds of their own, just like humans, and can be as stubborn or as sweet as we can. Do you remember a time when someone told you to do something and you didn't do it? While you heard and understood what was being asked, *you* were the one who decided whether you were going to comply or not. Animals are just like us: they have free will.

What do animals want humans to know about life?

Life is supposed to be fun and joyful. They love to hear us laugh and love to see us smile. They want their humans to be more peaceful and loving to one another, to all living creatures, and to Mother Earth. It doesn't get any simpler than that.

Are animals a reflection
of their humans?

U nequivocally, yes, animals are a reflection of their humans. I have also heard the terminology "mirroring" used to describe this phenomenon. Animals are very in-tune with their human's emotions and their behavior will often reflect their human's.

I communicated with a cat who told me that he wasn't grieving about the passing of his dog sibling because he was still able to communicate with the dog now in spirit form. The reason he was grieving, however, was because his human was so devastated by his dog sibling's death. Once she found peace and happiness, so would he.

I also had a horse communicate to me that he was frustrated with his human because she didn't "get in the zone" when riding him. Then his human told me that she was frustrated with the horse because he wouldn't "get into the zone" when she rode *him*. He used the same wording she did in our conversation, and he spoke the words to me before she did.

So, when you become frustrated with something your animal may be doing, step back, take a few deep breaths, and evaluate what is going on with you. In some cases, the animal is reflecting or mirroring *your* behavior.

Chapter 3: Hershey the Chocolate Lab

I had the pleasure of meeting Hershey in person, while he was being trained to become a service dog. His human wanted me to communicate with Hershey because she had a feeling he wasn't happy with the service dog training. Hershey's human had noticed that he didn't wag his tail like he used to and seemed bored with the whole training process. She wanted to know if there was something else he would rather do because she wanted him to be fulfilled.

I mentally asked Hershey if he was satisfied with his training or if there was something else he would rather do. Immediately, a scene of him chasing ducks in a large field filled my mind.

"I am a hunting dog. It's in my blood, and I get my hunting knowledge from my dad's bloodline," Hershey said.

I then saw another image in my head that looked like a magazine cover. I could see the words "Field & Stream," and there was a picture of Hershey holding a bird in his mouth standing next to a person. Hershey informed me that he was excellent at bird hunting and wanted to be outside chasing birds, hunting them, and teaching other dogs how to hunt. He expressed that he wanted to be on the cover of the magazine because he is such an intelligent dog who could share his knowledge with other dogs and humans. I felt the passion from Hershey when he was communicating. He was so serious; he would rather be a hunting dog than a service dog.

When I relayed this information to his human, I could sense her sadness to hear that he no longer wanted to be a service dog. It was bittersweet to know that Hershey had a different purpose in life that was incompatible with hers, but she seemed willing to rehome him so he could follow his passion.

One year later, Hershey's human updated me on his progress. He had been rehomed with a hunter and had taken to it like a fish to water. The hunter said Hershey was a born hunting dog and hadn't even needed much training. It was as if hunting was indeed in Hershey's blood. I started to laugh because this was *exactly* what Hershey had communicated to me. The woman told me he was a changed dog: tail wagging all the time, happy and fulfilled now that he had found his true purpose.

As of this writing I do not believe Hershey has been on a magazine cover, but it wouldn't surprise me if he does achieve this someday. I truly believe Hershey will be able to pursue his passions and accomplish his dreams because his human listened to his inner wants and needs and because he is such an amazing dog.

Chapter 4: Arthur the Doberman

I met Arthur and his two humans in person for their session. Arthur communicated to me that he doesn't like the "yucky stuff" being put on his food. His human informed me the "yucky stuff" was made of vitamins. She had stopped adding the supplements for 2 months but had just recently purchased a 10-pound bag of the vitamins and began putting it on his food again. Arthur asked if he could have a banana as a treat since he is having to take the "yucky stuff" on his food, and his human agreed.

Arthur told me he wanted a sweater. He kept showing me the colors green and yellow. Arthur's male human explained the colors as those of his favorite football team, the Green Bay Packers. Arthur informed me he would be okay wearing one of his sister's sweaters as long as it didn't have bows on it and hoped his humans could buy him his own sweater at the end of the winter. Both of his humans confirmed that his dog sisters had sweaters and that they had put one of these sweaters on him.

Arthur loved spending time with his male human while he watched television. Arthur's human told me that he does like to watch shows and that Arthur does indeed hang out with him when he watches.

Arthur showed me a picture of himself sitting in the front seat of an SUV and I heard the word "shotgun" in my head. His humans told me they did not own an SUV, but their daughter did and they confirmed that, yes, he does sit in the front seat.

Arthur's humans then asked if he liked his dog sisters and Arthur told me that he did like all 3 of his sisters. His humans seemed confused for a moment because they only had 2 female dogs and they couldn't understand where he was coming up with the third sister. After a couple of minutes, they both remembered his one true bloodline sister who lived with another family, so Arthur did in fact have 3 sisters.

Arthur had picked out his female human and it had been love at first sight. His human confirmed that she felt he did pick her out and that yes it was love at first sight.

I kept calling Arthur "beautiful," and he kept correcting me by telling me to use the word "handsome" because he is a male dog and not female. He went on to say that he wants to be a therapy dog when he gets older and visit senior citizens because they will appreciate him more than the younger generation.

Arthur showed me a picture of himself hanging out on the deck by the pool. He went on to say that the pool was closed way too early this year because the weather was still nice. His humans confirmed the existence of the pool where Arthur regularly hangs out on the deck as if he were the lifeguard, ready to jump in and save anyone who might be drowning.

Arthur liked the human friends who come over and visit. I heard him say: "They are fun but weird." His humans confirmed that they do have friends who are fun and they could see how Arthur might find them a bit strange.

Arthur communicated that he would do everything and anything to protect his female human. His human told me they took a guard dog class, but he refused to attack the volunteer "attacker" during the classroom training scenarios. Arthur said he didn't attack because it was in a controlled environment without true danger. He promised to use his last dying breath to protect his female human in a heartbeat. She should never doubt his ability to keep her safe from harm.

Arthur said he was NOT the sloppy drinker and asked for the water in his dish to not be so cold. Both of his humans laughed at this request because they had thought he was just messy!

Arthur showed me an issue with his right ear 6 months prior. His humans confirmed the issue and added that it had taken a while for it to get better.

I could feel the love and joy radiate from Arthur when we had our session. I also could feel how much his humans loved him. What a blessing for the humans and for Arthur to have a joyful and loving relationship.

Chapter 5: Ruby the Cocker Spaniel

Ruby is a 16-year-old cocker spaniel who was going to be departing her dog body soon due to health issues. I met Ruby and her humans in person a few days before she crossed over the rainbow bridge.

Ruby wanted her humans to remember all the good times they'd had. She showed me an image of a raccoon and communicated to me how she got into a fight with it (and won!). Her human told me she'd had an incident with a raccoon when she was younger, and Ruby still had a scar on her backside from the raccoon scratching her. When I looked at Ruby's scar she communicated that she'd gotten a piece of the raccoon, too!

Ruby enjoyed playing in the water at the lake. She showed me a picture of an orange toy and told me she was *really* good at retrieving from the water. Her humans confirmed that Ruby did indeed love visiting the lake, playing in the refreshing water, and retrieving the orange toy.

Ruby was okay with leaving this world and going to the other side. She said she'd had a really good life here and now she was ready for another adventure. She told me that Saint Francis of Assisi was waiting for her and would be on the other side of the rainbow bridge to greet her. Ruby wanted her humans to know she was not saying goodbye to them for good. This was just a "See you later!" because they will once again meet on the other side. She wanted her humans to be happy and remember all the fun times rather than focusing on the sad things about her life.

It was a true blessing to meet and communicate with Ruby before her departure from earth.

Chapter 6: Corkie the Miniature Pinscher

I met with Corkie to find out why she was having issues with not putting her tail up in the air when being shown for conformation. Corkie showed lots of confidence in the ring, but when it came time for judging she would not put her tail up in the air. Her human was becoming very frustrated and couldn't figure out what was going on, so she asked me if I would be able to find out the reason.

Corkie communicated to me that she did not like people looking at her behind, so she keeps her tail down. Her human wanted to know what she could do to encourage Corkie to get her tail up.

Corkie showed me an image of a dog wearing pajamas and insisted that she wanted pajamas, too.

I laughed to myself in disbelief, thinking to myself: "How am I going to tell her human that she wants pajamas?" I took a deep breath and told the woman her dog's deepest wish.

I honestly was expecting a weird look from Corkie's human, but she promised to purchase a pair of pajamas that very same day if Corkie promised to put her tail up in the ring.

It turned out the other dogs in the household wore pajamas, and Corkie was feeling left out. I told Corkie she would get her pajamas as soon as she put her tail up in the ring. Corkie didn't waste a minute and held her tail at attention. Her human didn't waste a minute either, and presented Corkie with her very own pair of pajamas that day.

Corkie's human later told me that Corkie seems so happy and content wearing the pajamas. Both human and dog have reached an understanding, and their relationship has grown to a new level.

It was a hoot speaking with Corkie. Some dogs just adore pajamas!

Chapter 7: Dakota the Rottweiler

Dakota's human contacted me to have a session with her deceased dog to make sure he was okay now that he had crossed over into the spirit world. When I started communicating with Dakota, I was shown a picture of the rainbow bridge and he was walking across it. I then heard him say: "Look who greeted me on the bridge."

Strangely enough, I visualized the fairy godmother, Glenda the Good Witch, from the Wizard of Oz. She wore a big, puffy pink dress, had a huge smile on her face, and was holding her magical wand. This was a new one for me because animals usually show me deceased loved ones, animals, religious figures, or saints.

When I told Dakota's human what I was seeing, she became quiet. She then proceeded to tell me that the family had watched the Wizard of Oz a couple of weeks before Dakota's passing, and he had been in the room when they watched it. Her youngest daughter was very interested in fairies and fairy godmothers (especially the one in the Wizard of Oz) and was also very attached to Dakota.

I got chills as she told me this. I truly felt this was Dakota's way of letting the family, especially the daughter, know he was okay and in a better place.

I then heard Dakota say: "There is plenty of food on this side." His human told me he was very interested in food and would wait for the humans to walk out of the room before trying to eat everything in sight. It made total sense to his human that he would tell her there was plenty of food there.

Dakota promised to send bright shiny quarters and cardinals to his humans as a sign to his humans to let them know he is still around them. His human told me she had just found 8 shiny quarters in her car that day and she had recently seen those same birds.

Dakota then added: "Tell mommy I have a squirrel here with me."

When Dakota was younger, there had been a squirrel nest, and he had gently brought the baby squirrels into his kennel inside the house. Dakota had gotten extremely upset when his human had taken the baby squirrels back outside for the mother squirrel to care for them.

Right before the end of our session Dakota showed me a huge bowl of popcorn that had lots and lots of butter on it. I then heard him say: "There is plenty of popcorn on this side." His human started laughing, confirming that the family had eaten buttered popcorn and shared it with Dakota.

I thought it was amazing Dakota showed me Glenda the Good Witch at the beginning of our session. He wanted to make sure his young human knew he was okay and that he was with someone she knew and loved. Now when I see Glenda the Good Witch, I will be reminded of my session with Dakota.

Chapter 8: Alberto the Horse

I had the honor and pleasure of communicating with a deceased horse named Alberto because his humans wanted to make sure he had safely crossed the rainbow bridge. When I asked Alberto if he was okay in spirit, he showed me a gigantic rainbow and told me that he was whole again.

Alberto then showed me a picture of him walking on water. I didn't really understand the image's meaning, but when I shared what I was being shown with his humans they became very emotional. They shared with me he had walked across a frozen body of water to rescue someone and he was usually afraid of ice. When he had managed to get the person to safety, they were amazed at his courage and bravery.

I then heard Alberto say: "I am the son of the man. He is my father." The man told me that he had a very special relationship with the horse and felt like Alberto was a son to him. Alberto then told me he knew how proud his human was of him and wanted to thank him for all that he had done for him while he was on earth.

Alberto wanted his humans to keep an eye out for the foxes on the property. His humans were dealing with a fox problem on their farm because the predators had been hunting and killing the chickens. Alberto told me that he was very observant and that his humans needed to be observant, too. His humans agreed: he was the most observant horse they had ever had.

Alberto added that they needed to watch out for the mice around the food. His humans hadn't yet noticed a problem with mice but would certainly keep their eyes open.

At the end of our session, Alberto showed me a picture of red hearts, showing his love for his humans while he was here on earth and his continual love now that he is in spirit form. He wanted them to know he was still around them and that he would be sending them cardinals as a sign from him. His humans promised to keep an eye out for the red birds.

It was an amazing session with Alberto and his humans. I could feel the love radiate from both parties during my time with them.

Chapter 9: Fresco the Horse

Fresco had just recently passed when I had a session with him and his human. His human wanted to make sure he was doing well transitioning from one life to the next and that he was alright with some of the decisions she had made after his passing.

Fresco showed me a picture of a horse dying suddenly out in a pasture. His human confirmed that this was how he had passed. I then heard Fresco say: "I saw her lean over me and cry on me." His human confirmed she had indeed behaved this way after his passing. Fresco communicated to me that he did not have any pain and that he went very quickly. He wanted to make sure his human knew this and did not feel guilt over his sudden passing.

Fresco had some very important things to say to his human: "I was here to teach you something about yourself, and my job was done. It was time for me to leave this earth, and there was nothing you could have done to stop it."

Fresco went on to show me an image of a forklift gently lowering his body into the ground. He said: "You put me in a hole and adjusted my body before you put dirt on me. I would like for you to plant some daisies or flowers on my grave. It's okay if you don't visit me because I am not really there. I am with you in spirit."

Fresco knew his tail hairs had been cut and made into a braid for his human to keep part of him with her for always. He noticed that his human smells items of his to remind her of him. His human said, yes, all of this was true.

Fresco showed me a picture of himself standing in a field of luscious green plants and wanted to let his human know he had lots of delicious grass to eat. He then showed me an image of a feather, and I didn't really understand the meaning of it, so I described it to his human. She informed me she *did* have a tattoo of a horse who looked just like Fresco wearing feathers on his head that she had gotten before she ever met him. (Fresco said the tattoo was of him whether she knew it or not!)

As we came to the end of our session, I heard these parting words from Fresco in my mind: "I love you and I am very proud of all the things you learned about yourself. You are a good student." The most important lesson Fresco had taught her, his human said, was patience.

Chapter 10: Abraham the Horse

One Sunday, I attended a cowboy church service with my sister. I had no idea what to expect!

When I arrived, I saw a preacher on a horse getting ready to give the sermon. While the service continued, I realized that the preacher's horse was looking directly at me. I then began to hear the horse ask me to speak to the preacher after the service. The preacher wore a small cross on the lapel of his jacket, and the horse wanted to wear the same symbol. He wanted people to respect him because he was also working for God delivering words of love and peace. The horse expressed that he was proud to be preaching the word of God with the man.

At the end of the service, I went and spoke with the preacher and told him what his horse, Abraham, had communicated to me. I told him how proud Abraham was to be a part of his mission to spread the word of God. I could feel Abraham's emotions as clearly as if they were my own.

The preacher was very kind to me and did not roll his eyes or make me feel uncomfortable, which sometimes happens when I explain my ability to others. My sister, who was with me that day, had wanted to run the other way. She kept telling me to just let it go and not embarrass myself because he was probably not going to believe a word I said.

The preacher told me Abraham *did* have the symbol of a cross on his saddle. At this moment, I heard Abraham tell me he wanted it on his halter, too, so that people could see it clearly during the services. So, I insisted on behalf of Abraham's wishes a second time.

The preacher promised to find a way to put the pin on the halter.

As I was walking away from the preacher I heard Abraham say: "Thank you and God Bless You."

Abraham was extremely proud of doing God's work with his human and wanted it to be more obvious to others!

Chapter 11: Thomas the Turtle

I met Thomas at a children's event and immediately felt a connection with him. I heard him say: "I'm hungry."

When I asked the human who had brought him to the event if she had fed him she responded: "Yes I just fed him."

I immediately heard him add: "Yeah, she gave me the light green lettuce. I want the dark green lettuce because I am not full."

I told the woman what Thomas communicated to me and she looked at me quizzically. She confirmed that she did indeed give him the light green lettuce. She then asked me, "How do you know I gave him light green lettuce?"

I told her that the turtle communicated it to me. She looked at me very strangely and said she would give him some dark lettuce when they got back to the center. As I was walking away, I heard the turtle express his gratitude.

It was my pleasure to be able to verbalize Thomas' desire for the dark lettuce to his human.

Chapter 12: George the Fish

One day, when I was at a woman's house for a gathering, a fish aquarium caught my eye and I walked over to see one of the fish wildly swimming around, desperately trying to get someone's attention. I asked him why he was so agitated.

The fish communicated to me that his friend had recently died and he wanted a new friend that looked like him. He expressed his sadness that all the other animals in the tank had a friend except him. I told the woman what the fish wanted, and she confirmed that the other species of fish like him had died a few days before, but had not been replaced yet. She promised to find another fish like him so he would be happier.

A couple of weeks later when I stopped by the woman's house I checked in with the fish. I saw that he had a new fish friend that looked just like him in the tank. I heard George tell me, "I am much happier now because I have a friend that looks like me." It also appeared as if George was smiling at me when I was listening to him. Friendship and companionship are very important, even to fish!

Chapter 13: Lucy the Sheep

I met Lucy when I volunteered at a sheep therapy program for children. Throughout the program, the kids learned how to wash and dry the sheep; dress them up in fancy scarves, hats, and boas; and then walk them around the farm using a lead.

One day, the child I was working with decided to dress Lucy up in blue accessories. The child was laughing and having a good time, and I said to the child that the sheep looked beautiful in her attire.

I then heard Lucy say, "I look ridiculous."

I responded by saying out loud, "You don't look ridiculous. You look beautiful and are bringing us so much joy."

Lucy turned her head, looked up at me, and asked if I could understand her. My response was: "Yes, I can hear you." She stared at me for a few seconds in disbelief. It was then I realized that all animals don't know they can communicate with humans.

When we walked Lucy back to the barn, I heard her yelling to the other sheep: "You are not going to believe this but this lady can understand us and talk to us." As soon as she said it, all the other sheep turned their heads to look at me.

They were not looking at anyone else in the barn, just me. At that moment, I realized that word gets around fast in the barnyard!

Chapter 14: Ace the Labradoodle

I had the pleasure of chatting with Ace, his human, and her sister via telephone. His human contacted me because she had a few questions for Ace.

The first question she wanted to know was why he was no longer eating the dental chews that she gave him. When I asked Ace about the dental chews, he replied: "They taste like crap. I don't want to eat them. They are horrible." According to his human, these chews were the same ones he had always been given, but Ace insisted: "I think they have changed the formula or something as they taste like crap." His human said she would look into it for him.

Ace's human wanted to know where he came from. He showed me a picture of a puppy being dumped out by the road in the country and him walking alongside of it. When I communicate with animals, I usually only ask for them to show me good things. If they have had a rough life or if bad things happened to them, I do not want to have the negative images in my head. But in this case, Ace's story had a happy ending.

Ace had just appeared at the human's doorstep one day when he was a puppy. Ace informed me that he had found his forever home, and it didn't matter where he came from. It only mattered that he was safe now with his human who had taken him in and loved him for the past 6 years.

Ace then communicated to me that he *loved* scrambled eggs with cheese. His human told me, "He doesn't get those." I then saw a picture of Ace licking his lips and heard him say, "I love scrambled eggs with cheese." Again, his human said she did not give him any eggs.

Just then the sister of his human said: "Uhm, I give him scrambled eggs with cheese and yes he does love it." His human was very surprised by this because she'd had no idea her sister was sneaking him the scrumptious dish.

Ace told me that there was a female dog in the house who he called his "sweetie." I told his human I felt like this dog was a dog friend, but not a romantic dog girlfriend. His human told me that there was another dog in the house who was female and that they were indeed friends.

But a couple of days after our session, I got an email from his human saying: "When you asked if there was a girl dog who could possibly be Ace's sweetie, I thought our lab was the female dog he was talking about. After thinking about it, I realized he was probably talking about our dog who had recently passed away. Her name was Sweetie, and he did love playing with her!" I got chills when I read the note.

As our session was coming to an end, Ace told me: "I do not like having bows in my hair."

The women started laughing and I heard Ace's aunt say to her sister, "I told you he doesn't like them!" His human then told me that she does not put bows in his hair, but barrettes. She said that Ace has longer hair on the top of his head and she would clip it away from his face so he could see better. She also said sometimes the groomer put barrettes in his hair.

Then Ace showed me a picture of Bono from the group U2. I didn't know what this meant so I asked the ladies, "Do you like the group U2, or is there some significance with Bono for you?" They both told me no that it didn't have any meaning to them.

I then heard in my head these words from Ace. "Bono would never have bows or barrettes in his hair. I am a male dog and males do not wear bows or barrettes. I look ridiculous with them in my hair. It is humiliating. Cut my hair shorter and don't put those in my hair anymore."

Both his human and his aunt were laughing hysterically. His human agreed not put them in his hair anymore and would get the hair on top of his head cut shorter.

Ace then communicated to me, "And I want my beard cut shorter. It's a real pain and makes a mess." His human told me that she loved his beard and usually told the groomer not to cut it. Ace didn't like the long facial hair and wanted it to be shorter, so she agreed to follow his wishes.

Ace showed me that animals can be as fashion conscious as humans!

Chapter 15: King the Dog

King's human reached out to me because he was concerned that King wasn't eating his food. She had already taken him to the vet, and the vet said he appeared to be in good physical health. When I communicated with King, he said: "There is nothing wrong with me. I am not eating my food because I do not like the food. I want different food."

He then showed me a picture of what appeared to me to be wet food. His human confirmed that she was currently feeding him dry food and that she would look into changing his food.

During our session King also showed me a picture of a stuffed yellow duck. In words, he said: "The duck is my favorite toy, and it is stuck underneath the recliner." His human confirmed that he did have a stuffed yellow duck and that she hadn't seen it in a while because she didn't know where he'd hidden it.

A week after our session, King's human contacted me with a follow-up. She had changed King's diet, and he was eating again like normal. She'd also found the yellow duck! It was exactly where King said it was: under the recliner. King began carrying the duck around in his mouth again and appeared to be a much happier dog.

Occasionally everyone needs a little help from their friends.

Chapter 16: Yippee and Skippee the Terriers

I had the pleasure of communicating with two terriers and I kept hearing the words "Yippee and Skippee" in my head. I didn't even remember being told their real names, so when I heard those words I turned to their human and said, "Are their names Yippee and Skippee?"

The look on her face was absolutely priceless. Her mouth was wide open and her eyes were *huge*. I think she was in a little bit of shock.

"How do you know those names?" she asked me.

"The dogs are communicating to me, and they told me the names," I replied.

Their human told me Yippee and Skippee were not the dogs' real names, but their nicknames. Their human wanted to know if they were okay with their real names and I was shown a picture in my head along with the word "Yes."

Skippee showed me his bad teeth and communicated that he knew his human didn't want to spend the money on him right now to get them cleaned. His human nodded in agreement.

Yippee told me that if his human had any doubts about taking them to the groomer, then she shouldn't do it. Their human confided in me that she was thinking of not taking them to the same groomer again. Yippee knew she was considering it, and both dogs were in favor of the change.

Skippee showed me an image of a groomer smoking in the same area with the dogs while they were being groomed. "She loves to gossip and she really doesn't take good care of us while we are there," he said.

The groomer had cut them both a couple of times, and their human confirmed that this had worried her. At the end of our session the woman informed me that she was definitely *never* going to use that careless groomer again!

It was comforting to know that their human believed their story and wanted to see that they were well taken care of.

Chapter 17: Deputy the Horse

I had a phone session with a horse named Deputy and his human because his human wondered what was causing him to spook when they rode by a particular section of the woods near his barn.

Deputy kept showing me images of guns being shot. I asked his human if people hunted in the wooded area where they went riding. His human replied that dove hunting season had just begun, but the spooking had started months ago.

I asked Deputy again what was spooking him, and again he kept showing me pictures of guns shooting. I kept hearing "pop, pop, pop" in my head similar to gunfire, so I explained this to Deputy's human.

At first the human didn't understand this noise, and then she realized its meaning. Just recently, the nearby lumberyard had been under construction and the workers had used nail guns to put on the new roof. Bingo! I got chills all over my body, and I could see the horse shaking his head up and down confirming what she was saying. Deputy told me that the woods were really dense and that the popping noise was really loud.

Deputy's human planned to work with him to get over his fears and promised that they would not be riding near those woods during hunting season. I could feel a huge weight being lifted off my shoulders when Deputy heard what I was saying.

At the end of our session, Deputy told me that he and his human had come to a new road. He was confident they would have an even better relationship and understanding of one another. It really helped to have his human listen to the details he was giving so they could work through the issue together.

Chapter 18: Rocky the Horse

One day while volunteering at a barn, I had a gut feeling that I needed to walk down to the end of the aisle and visit a horse there. When I reached the last stall, I encountered Rocky.

Rocky wanted me to tell the veterinarian, who was currently working in the barn, that he would "see him tomorrow." It turned out the vet had been called out that day to check on this horse because he was having some health issues.

The vet didn't know me and would probably think I was crazy. But Rocky was extremely persistent, so I eventually approached the vet and delivered the message. Needless to say, the vet looked at me *very* strangely.

Honestly, I think the vet thought I was totally off my rocker. He didn't answer me, but the look on his face said it all. After a minute or two, the vet then said it would not be a good thing if he had to come back out here tomorrow because it would mean things were getting worse for Rocky.

The following day I found out that the barn manager had called the vet at 8am to ask him to come back out to the barn. Only this time it was not for Rocky, but for another horse who was having some health issues.

Rocky was indeed correct in saying he would "see the vet tomorrow." He had conveniently left out the part where the vet wouldn't be coming to the barn to see him but instead would be coming out to see a different horse.

I have come to realize animals can be extremely humorous. I wouldn't be surprised if Rocky laughed about the whole scenario for days and weeks afterward!

Chapter 19: Abby the Dog

Abby's human contacted me to find out how she was feeling, and we completed our session over the phone while I looked at a picture of the dog.

The photo of Abby I had been given was a close-up of her face. I could not see her legs or the back half of her body, which Abby's human had done deliberately to see if I would know about her dog's disability. The woman said she didn't know if she really believed in "all of this animal communication stuff" and wanted to see what I knew without seeing Abby fully.

When I first saw Abby's sweet face, she said: "I can't walk very well. My legs don't work right." In my head, I saw an image of a dog wheelchair and heard the word "wheelies."

I told the woman what Abby had said, and the woman responded: "You are really freaking me out with this."

I asked if I was incorrect, and she said "No." The dog *was* indeed having issues with walking and she *was* considering getting a set of "wheelies" for Abby to use, but didn't know if that was something Abby wanted or if she would rather try to correct the problem with surgery.

Abby communicated to me that she did *not* want to have surgery. She did not want to spend her time recovering from a surgery at fifteen years old and said that she wasn't going to live forever. She preferred the wheelies because she wanted to have fun and joy in her life right now instead of experiencing pain in her remaining days.

I must give full credit to Abby for communicating to me what was going on with her legs. I am just the messenger giving the messages from the animals. Great job to Abby for knowing exactly what she wants from life!

Chapter 20: Pumpkin the Rescue Dog

Pumpkin immediately started talking to me: "I just want to be her dog. I don't want to be the dog known as being raised in a cage in horrible conditions. I don't want the stigma of it. I just want to be her dog. I don't want people to feel sorry for me. I want to feel happy and just want to be known as her dog."

His human confirmed that she did tell people he was a rescue dog and that he'd had a rough life in the past. After hearing what Pumpkin was communicating, she told me she would make a better effort to stop telling people about his past and would start introducing him "as the best dog she has ever had" to people.

Pumpkin had a very quiet and mellow energy, but he also had a serious side. "Don't ever doubt that I won't protect my human. If something were to happen I would be right there to protect her from it," he told me.

His human was concerned about his lack of appetite. But the dog communicated to me that there was something going on in his human's life and that *her* appetite had decreased as well. As I have said before, animals are reflections of humans. Pumpkin knew his human had been sad lately and was under a lot of stress. His human confirmed these feelings.

Pumpkin then communicated: "I am not going anywhere. I am not dying anytime soon. I have a good life. My house is my kingdom, so please do not worry that I am going to pass away any time soon." His human had been concerned about his loss of appetite and worried that she might have to release him from his physical body soon.

Lately, Pumpkin had been acting quite nervous. He explained that his human was worrying about every little detail in her life, and that this was where he was picking up the emotion. Pumpkin wanted to be a happy dog and he wanted his human to be happy also.

Pumpkin had a recommendation for his human: "If you want me to be less nervous take a couple of deep breaths and tell yourself things are all good."

Pumpkin then showed me a picture of a game they used to play together and said he wanted to play it again. I saw a scene of a ball or sock thrown down a long hallway, a game his human confirmed they used to play, but that it had been years since they had.

Pumpkin wanted his human to laugh more. He remembered a time when she would laugh so hard she almost peed her pants and he missed her happiness. His human promised to make an effort to find joy now that he had brought it to her attention.

Pumpkin loved going on car rides and showed me a picture of himself riding in the front seat. He said, "I am her copilot. She talks a lot to herself in the car, and I think it's funny. She is always missing the turns and we get lost a lot." His human began laughing and agreed that all of this was true.

Pumpkin then showed me a jar of peanut butter. I asked his human if she gives him peanut butter, and she said she used to give him this treat but doesn't anymore. Pumpkin spoke up right away: "Ask her why she doesn't give me peanut butter? Just because I don't have all my teeth doesn't mean I can't enjoy some peanut butter. Let her know I would like to have some peanut butter."

I then saw Pumpkin licking his lips. I told his human his request, and she laughed out loud saying she would make sure he got some.

As the session came to an end, Pumpkin added: "We get up way too early. She gets up at 3am and that is *much* too early. I am not able to get a full night of sleep." His human laughed and shook her head and said, yes, she does get up around 3am and can't get right back to sleep. She couldn't believe Pumpkin was bringing this up in our session. I told her this was his opportunity to bring up things that were important to him, and he had a lot to say to his human!

I think Pumpkin's motto could be summed up as "don't worry be happy."

Chapter 21: Sammy the Labradoodle

When I chatted with Sammy, the first thing she showed me was a yellow stuffed toy that looked like a banana. This was her favorite and she loved running around the house with it in her mouth. Her human explained that she *did* carry around a yellow stuffed toy, but it was an ear of yellow corn, not a banana. Usually animals show me images of things I can understand so they may not be exact but the humans generally make the connection.

Sammy said she spends too much time in her crate, so she chews on the metal door. Her human agreed.

Sammy loved to lick her human's feet after she got a pedicure. Her human said to me, "Oh my gosh how do you know she does that? I haven't shared it with anyone because I just think it's so gross!"

I replied: "Well your dog just told me, so that's how I know."

Sammy's human wanted me to ask *why* in the world Sammy licked her toes.

She said: "Her feet are nice and clean, and I want to put my smell on them so other dogs know she is my human."

Before the end of our session, I asked Sammy if she had anything else she wanted to talk about, and she told me she wanted to sleep right beside her human's bed. Her human had been thinking about having her sleep there, but didn't know if Sammy would like it. Now knowing Sammy's wishes, she promised to put a dog bed beside the human bed so Sammy could sleep closer to her human.

At the end of our session I felt there was a much better understanding between Sammy and her human.

Chapter 22: Coco the Chocolate Lab

Coco's family reached out to me because they were concerned about her low weight.

When I began communicating with Coco, she thought it was funny that they were concerned about her being thin and not really concerned about her dog sibling being too large. Coco did not use the word "fat" to describe her sibling. Numerous animals have told me that they do not like the word fat. It did not surprise me that Coco used the term "large" instead. Coco communicated to me she was just a thin dog and that they shouldn't spend their time focusing on size.

Next, Coco showed me a picture of a blue baby pool with a crack in it. "I want to have the baby pool again. They put it away and haven't brought it back out. I want to play in the pool again," she said, and her human confirmed the baby pool had been put away.

She showed me an image of her circling in the water three times and then flopping down with a splash. "I would like to have the pool out today," she said, insistently repeating this phrase several times more until her human agreed to set up the pool that same day.

A few hours after talking to Coco, I got an update from her human: she had gotten the baby pool out for Coco. When the pool was full, Coco circled three times and flopped down in it, just like she'd showed me.

That day Coco got her wish! And she and her human were on their way to building a stronger bond.

Chapter 23: Frankie the Greyhound

I had the pleasure of meeting a rescued greyhound named Frankie. His human wanted to know if he missed his dog sibling who had passed away and if he would like to have a new sibling.

Frankie expressed that even though his sibling was no longer there in dog form, he was still able to communicate with him in spirit form. When I asked Frankie if he would like to have another sibling his response was "No." He wanted to be the only dog and spend lots of quality time with his human one-on-one.

Frankie showed me a picture of himself sleeping on the bed like a human with his head on a pillow. His human confirmed that Frankie *did* sleep on the bed, and sometimes he put his head on the pillow, but mainly sprawled out over the king-size bed. (After our session, Frankie's human emailed me a picture of Frankie sleeping in the middle of the bed, upside-down with his legs sticking straight up.)

Frankie then showed me a bag of light brown cookies and communicated to me that he enjoyed eating them. His human had given him these treats in the past, but it had been a while. Frankie wanted her to know he *did* enjoy those cookies and would like to eat them again.

Next, Frankie said two words that made me laugh: "Dr. Phil".

"Do you watch Dr. Phil?" I asked his human.

"Yes, we do watch Dr. Phil! Every day at 3pm Frankie and I sit in the living room and watch it."

"See, I told you we watched Dr. Phil. It wasn't your imagination," said Frankie.

I wonder if Dr. Phil knows his audience members include animals!

Chapter 24: Maggie the Bird

I had the pleasure of meeting a beautiful white bird named Maggie in person. When I started my session with her, the first thing she showed me was a picture of a red apple.

I asked her human if she fed Maggie apples, and she confirmed that she *did* feed her the fruit on a regular basis. Maggie had even been fed apples that day. But when her human offered another piece, Maggie had refused to take it.

Maggie showed me the picture of the red apple three more times.

"I don't know what this means, but she keeps showing me a piece of apple with red skin," I said.

Maggie's human told me she doesn't give her the skin of the apple because of the toxins.

Again, Maggie showed me a picture of a red apple. I tried to sort out why Maggie insisted on the color red, so I asked her human what color apples she had given the bird lately.

"You are really freaking me out! That apple *was* a green apple because my husband bought the wrong kind the other day," said Maggie's human.

Finally, it all made perfect sense! Maggie likes red apples, *not* green, and that's why she kept insisting on the red apple.

At the end of our session, I asked Maggie if I could have a picture taken with her. She said, "Yes! I will do my Marilyn Monroe pose."

I laughed because I had no idea what she meant and neither did her human. Maggie perched on my shoulder with her white feathers standing straight up. Maggie told me she was posing this way so she looked just like Marilyn Monroe's famous photo of her wearing the white dress blowing in the wind. When I was a kid, my father loved Marilyn Monroe, and I inherited the famous photo of her wearing the white dress. Now when I look at the photo, I think of Maggie and smile.

(And going forward Maggie will always get her red apples!)

Chapter 25: Bobby the Cocker Spaniel

I met Bobby in person when I visited my friend's niece. When we walked in the door, Bobby came right over to smell me and he kept repeating: "I am a police dog. I am a police dog."

I thought this odd and amusing because I don't think I had *ever* seen a cocker spaniel as a police dog before. When I told his human this, her mouth dropped open. It turned out that Bobby's nickname was "The Sherriff," and he often wore a star-shaped badge his humans had given him.

Bobby's human said she was having some issues with him barking at a couple of people. Bobby informed me that his human didn't appear to like these people and he was only telling them to leave because they were not welcome in the house. When I relayed this to his human, her face was quizzical. After a few moments, she agreed with the dog.

After the visit, I was invited to stay for dinner. When we sat down to eat, Bobby sat at my feet and barked at me.

Now you might be thinking he was telling me I was not welcome. But what he was actually saying was: "You are the only one who can understand me. I want some food!"

This made me laugh out loud. I informed him I didn't have any food to give him. After he realized I was serious about not giving him food, he quit barking and laid down for the rest of our visit.

After our session, I came to realize that any dog can be a protective "police dog."

Chapter 26: Felix the Cat

Felix's humans didn't have any particular concerns they wanted to address. They just wanted to know what was on his mind.

When I first looked at Felix's picture my thought was, "My you are a big boy." I do not use the words fat or obese in my sessions. Animals do NOT like being called overweight, fat, or obese.

"I am *not* fat!" said Felix.

His body was overflowing from the human's hands that were holding him in the photograph. I apologized for thinking that thought about him, and then he said, "Okay I accept your apology."

As I looked at Felix's picture, I could feel his energy and it felt like he was frustrated or ticked off about something. I asked Felix what was going on with him and if there was anything he wanted to share. He didn't waste a minute in communicating with me.

"She is feeding my food to another animal and I do not like it," Felix said.

I turned to his human and asked her if she was feeding his food to another animal. She replied, "There are no other animals in the house." But he repeated himself three times, and she denied it each time.

I couldn't figure out what was going on because I was getting two different stories, but I could feel the passion in Felix's words. I sat quietly for a moment hoping this scenario would be figured out. I was getting this information so strongly from Felix that I knew there had to be some truth to his words.

Felix's human finally admitted that there had been a feral cat approaching the door to look inside. But when the cat visited, she put Felix in another room and secretly fed it. She had a feeling Felix disliked the feral cat. When I asked what she was feeding the cat, she said it was the same food she fed Felix. Bingo! His human did not agree that this was what Felix was complaining about.

"I put him in another room. How could he possibly know I am feeding the feral cat?" she said.

I explained to her that animals know a lot more things than we give them credit for, and this was a perfect example.

Felix added, "She is feeding all the hobos and the carpet baggers that show up at our house with my food. It's like we are the food pantry for wild animals, and I do not like it."

His human said she didn't feed *every* stray animal, but she felt sorry for this cat and would feed it outside because she would not allow it in the house. Felix communicated to me that he did not want to share his food with anyone and he wanted her to stop feeding it.

Felix then told me he was done talking to me. He felt he had made it loud and clear to his human what he wanted and refused to speak anymore. Drop the mic!!!

Chapter 27: Duke the Rottweiler-Mix

I had the honor of communicating with Duke after he passed. His human wanted to make sure he was settling into his new afterlife.

Duke communicated to me in images that he crossed over the rainbow bridge and that his human's grandmother had met him over there. "Grandma really loved animals when she was on earth and she is the one who greeted me," he said.

His human's grandmother had passed over 30 years ago and she had really loved animals. Duke showed me a picture of himself sitting in a field of daisies as a woman stood beside him. Duke's human then told me that her grandmother's nickname was Daisy. As she said this I got chills all over me, signaling that what was being said in that moment was exactly what the animal wanted me to know. Duke did not show me a field of tall grass or cat tails or roses, he showed me a flower that had a double meaning.

Duke did not want his human to have any guilt over his death: "It was my time to go and my job on earth was done. It was time for me to go on my adventure."

His human admitted that she'd had a thought that perhaps her life would be easier without Duke, but then took it back immediately. The dog passed away within 24 hours of this thought.

Duke insisted that she did *not* cause his passing and even laughed saying, "You humans think you have so much power. You cannot cause someone to die just by a thought. You may think so but that isn't how it works. My time was done here, and you had nothing to do with it. I don't want you to have any guilt about it because it will make you sick. Release the guilt and continue to have a good life."

Duke showed me a picture of his human's feet on the bed, and his human confirmed that Duke used to sleep by her feet. Duke then said, "Even though I am no longer in my dog body and am now in spirit form, I still sleep on her bed." Sometimes she would be able to feel warmth in the area where he'd slept.

Duke showed me the word "patrol" and an image of him guarding the house. His human confirmed that he did "patrol" the house before they went to bed when he was alive. He still watches over the house in spirit form.

Duke then gave me a view of the yin and yang symbol and communicated to me that dog and human were like two peas in a pod. His human did feel like they were like the yin and yang, two opposite sides of the same coin.

Duke wanted his human to take comfort in how he passed. She did not have to make a decision to have him put down because his passing was not traumatic or full of pain or sickness. He had passed away in his sleep in his own home. Duke's exact words were, "I was sent here to be with you and help you with things in your life. My job was done here and it was time for me to go and start my new life on the other side. Please don't be sad about my passing. Please remember all the good times we had and know I am still around you in spirit and I love you very much."

At the end of our session Duke's human told me that she finally felt at peace with his passing.

Chapter 28: Gracie the Sheepdog-Poodle-Mix

Gracie is a sheepdog-poodle-mix who I met in person. At the start of our session she showed me a picture of the number eight. Sometimes animals show me a number when we begin a session and my interpretation of the number usually means one of these things: the animal's age, the number of homes an animal has had, or a date of some kind.

I asked if Gracie was 8 months old. Her human told me she was 1 year old and had been born in August, the eighth month of the year. I then heard Gracie say, "I am really smart and I got it from my dad who is really, really, really smart." Gracie's human said that her dad was a standard poodle and that, yes, he was really smart.

Gracie had picked out her human as a puppy. Even though the human and her husband went back and forth on whether to take Gracie home or not, the dog always knew they would be her family.

Gracie showed me an image of her holding a stick in her mouth. "I posed for the picture of me holding the stick," she said, and her human showed me this photo.

Gracie told me that she is the princess of the house and that there are no other animals in the house. Her human said, yes, she was the only animal and she was like a child to them. The dog wanted her human parents to know she loved them *very* much.

Gracie then showed me the words "new collar." I asked her human if she had gotten a new collar recently, she said she hadn't yet but was considering it because the current one seemed too tight. Gracie said she wanted a princess collar.

"I like scrambled eggs," Gracie said next. Her human told me that she did not usually feed the dog scrambled eggs, but her husband made them on Saturday mornings. Gracie licked her lips and repeated "I like scrambled eggs". Her human promised to give her a nibble the next time Saturday morning rolled around.

Gracie went on to tell me her love of ice cubes. Her human had just dropped an ice cube earlier that day and Gracie had picked it up to play with it.

"You are really freaking me out because you are spot on with so many things," Gracie's human said.

I laughed and replied, "I am just the messenger. The animals are the ones with the message."

Gracie went on to say: "I do *not* want my toenails painted *ever* and I don't like having my nails trimmed." Her human said that she was going to the dog salon in a couple of days and would be sure to tell the groomer about her preferences about her nails. Her human said she cut the hair over Gracie's eyes and thought she could see better. Gracie told me to thank her for trimming her hair because agreed she could see *much* better now.

Gracie communicated to me that she would like more exercise than just walking. "I'm really smart," she said. "I want to do something fun and energetic."

I asked Gracie if she would like to have some dog puzzles, and she communicated to me that she wanted something physical to do, like duck chasing, herding, or agility. Gracie's human promised to find a way for Gracie to use her smart mind and work off excess energy.

Gracie showed me a picture of peanut butter and her licking her lips at the same time. Her human said she did not get this treat, but Gracie knew where the treats were and *did* lick her lips when she wanted a treat.

Gracie laughingly told me: "I like to stop and smell things on my walks and pee on everything even if I only have a drop left." Gracie's human confirmed this and also laughed.

A couple of days later after our session I got a note from Gracie's human.

"Hi Cindy," she wrote. "I took Gracie on a walk after our reading, and as I was walking it just popped into my head: this past weekend when my husband and I were talking about whether the reading was going to be 'real,' we were joking and playing with Gracie's toenails. I said, if she tells us in the reading to stop touching her toenails, then we will know. I am positive that's why she kept telling you about her toenails and that she doesn't want them touched (or painted), which seemed so bizarre at the time, but now makes perfect sense!"

"I, of course, had to double-check my memory with my husband when he got home just to make sure I wasn't inventing it, and he confirmed we definitely had that conversation! Crazy! *And*, the other thing I wasn't sure about...the peanut butter! We remembered we actually used to give her doggy peanut butter bones all the time, and haven't gotten them for her in a while, I bet that's what she wanted!"

It never ceases to amaze me how much an animal will divulge to me once they know I can hear them.

Chapter 29: Riley the English Springer Spaniel

At the start of the session, Riley showed me the number 8. I asked her human if she was 8 years old, and her human said that her birthday was coming up and that she would indeed be turning eight.

Riley communicated to me she was a princess, and her human laughed. She said she didn't give Riley this title, but she could see how Riley would think she was a princess.

"I love chicken. I like peanut butter, but I really love chicken," Riley said. She added that she did *not* like the male vet telling her she was overweight and had to cut down on the chicken. Her human confirmed that they had just been to a male vet and that, yes, he had said these things. He'd said Riley should eat less "people food," which included chicken. No wonder Riley didn't like the vet!

Riley's human asked if she wanted to have another dog in the house. Riley replied, "No! I don't want another animal in the house. I want to spend more time with my mommy."

In the photo from our session, I noticed Riley was wearing a choke collar. When I asked about it, Riley confessed that she liked to pull when she went on walks because there was so much to see and smell.

Riley now had a harness and was no longer pulling so much on their walks. Riley showed me a picture of a red harness and her human nodded in agreement.

Riley expressed that she is really intelligent and wants to use her brain more. She wanted her human to hide things in the yard for her to find. Riley has a really good nose for smelling and loved to smell things.

Riley had a plan to get chicken back in her diet. She promised to play hide-and-seek in the backyard and get more exercise so she could eat her favorite foods again. Her human told me that she did play hide and seek with her inside the house, but Riley said: "No let's do it outside so I can run more and then I can have more chicken."

I laughed and thought to myself, "What a smart dog."

Chapter 30: Yoda the Dog

Yoda's human reached out to me for a session because she wanted to know if Yoda would like a dog companion in the house. Yoda replied loud and clear: "Hell no!"

Before I told his human his response, I asked her, "Do you curse?"

There was a moment of silence, and then she said, "Yes, sometimes. Why do you ask?"

My response was, "Well animals are a reflection of their humans, and if the human swears, it's more likely that the animal will, too. Your dog just swore but I didn't want to repeat it if you don't."

"What did Yoda say?" she laughed.

"He told me HELL NO he doesn't want another dog in the house," I said with a smile.

Yoda's human just burst out laughing. She then wanted to know if he was having hip issues because she'd had his hips checked out about a year ago.

"It is more of a pain in the ass ache," he responded, going on to say that his human worried too much and that she needed to relax. He said he wasn't going anywhere anytime soon. They should focus on having more fun and not his hips!

Yoda's human wanted to know if he liked his food or if there was something else going on with his health because he wasn't eating as much as he used to. I always tell people that I am *not* a vet. If there is ever a question about a health issue, I recommend they take their animal to see a health professional. Yoda told me that his food was different and he didn't like the taste.

"Throw that shit away and buy a new bag of food," he said with brutal honesty.

When I asked Yoda about his favorite treats, he showed me an image of a treat that looked like beef jerky or a Slim Jim. His human said she fed him "Pupperoni" sticks, but he didn't seem to be eating them. Yoda's response was: "They taste like shit. Throw them away. You are buying me the cheap stuff." His human confirmed that she had been buying cheaper treats at a different store.

Again, Yoda said: "Quit buying that shit at the dollar store. Food from the dollar store is *not* good. It's crap. Go to a different store and buy me better food."

At that, we laughed so hard our sides hurt!

Yoda communicated that he was *not* a morning dog. When his human got up at 4am to get ready for work, Yoda would just look at her as if to say, "Why are we getting up so early?" He would definitely like to sleep in later.

Yoda's human wanted to know if he liked his cat siblings in the house. "Oh, they are just cats," he replied. "They don't bother me. But I don't want another dog in this house."

When Yoda rode in the car with his human, he felt like the copilot. Though his human said she didn't bring him in the car often, she agreed that this was true. He was anticipating their Christmas road trip soon. Yoda wished his human would pay more attention to the road and said: "Sometimes I wish I could drive the car instead of her." His human admitted she sometimes made quick turns that unseated Yoda.

He showed me a picture of him rolling his eyes as he said: "Yeah, that is why I want to be in the driver's seat so I could hang on to the steering wheel." I immediately got goosebumps.

As the session came to a close, Yoda said he liked chatting with me because I went with the flow and didn't hold back on his thoughts and opinions. The last animal communicator he had spoken to was "tightly wound and didn't really express his attitude," and his human agreed.

Before our session ended, Yoda's human promised she would *definitely* buy him new food and new treats.

Yoda did not sugarcoat his opinions. Sometimes the best approach is being direct and to the point.

Chapter 31: Brando the Dachshund

When I started the session with Brando, he repeatedly said, "I am handsome! I am handsome!" Many humans, family, friends, and even strangers, often told Brando this.

His human asked if he was guarding the house when he walked around the house with his head held high. But Brando told me that he just enjoyed walking around the house telling himself he was handsome.

"I have a really good heart," he said, meaning physically and emotionally. His human seemed relieved to hear this because he'd had a heart test several years back and she was always concerned about it. Brando wanted her to know he wouldn't be leaving her anytime soon.

Brando told me he had a "pheasant friend," which baffled his owner because she had only seen turkeys in the yard. But Brando insisted, repeating the word "pheasant." His human said she would keep an eye out for it.

Brando asked for the winter blanket to come out for the season. He explained that he was starting to get cold, so his human promised to put it back on the bed after the session. He wanted someone to make him a "red sweater" because he wanted to be warm when he went outside, too. His human had been trying to find someone to make a custom coat for him, but had been unsuccessful so far. She promised to look harder!

Brando showed me an image of him with ribbons, and I asked the woman if he was a show dog. She said, no, but that they often attended rabbit hunting events. The event coming up was going to be bigger and better than what they had attended before and he was excited. His human confirmed that the previous weekend they had gone to a hunting event and he had done an amazing job competing. If he continued what he was doing, he would get his championship ribbon. I got chills as she told me this. Brando seemed very confident he would win!

I got a vision of Brando wearing a tie, and when I asked his human, she told me that he has a charm in the shape of a tie on his collar. He explained he had several different leashes in many colors, and depending on what sort of mood his human was in determined what color he wore. She just laughed and said she really hadn't paid attention to how she picked his leash but would be more observant.

Brando was a very fashion-forward (and handsome) fellow!

Chapter 32: Barkley the Mixed-Breed Dog

I immediately started calling Barkley "Buddy." At the end of the session, his human said that he found it interesting when I gravitated toward this name because the name at his previous home had been "Buddy."

The first thing Barkley wanted to communicate was that he liked to sit up front when they ride in the car as he was the co-pilot. "We get lost a *lot*. We drive around in circles a *lot*." he said. His human confirmed this and added that his poor sense of direction was actually a running joke in his workplace.

Barkley really liked the blonde woman his human talked to on the phone. "I think she is funny," he said. This turned out to be his human's mother. Barkley then showed me an image of a human rubbing his belly and said, "I *love* belly rubs." His human laughed and agreed that this was the case.

Barkley had taken a plane ride with his human and said he was placed under the seat. He seemed happy that they had gotten pretzels on the plane and *not* peanuts as a snack. His human explained Barkley's love of pretzels. After the plane ride, Barkley told me he really liked walking out in the woods with his human. Barkley showed me pictures of trails, which confused his human for a moment until he remembered that, after the pretzel-filled flight, they *had* visited a human friend who lived in a wooded area and had taken lots of walks.

I never cease to be amazed by the amount of information animals remember!

Chapter 33: Felicity the Horse

Right from the start, Felicity took charge of the communication. I could feel a very strong energy coming from her.

"I am a spit fire. I am very stubborn and strong-willed and my daddy is more cooperative," the horse said. Felicity's human agreed with everything Felicity communicated to me, including that Felicity's sire (her father) lived on the farm with them.

Felicity communicated to me that her human was trying to teach her something, but she didn't quite understand what it was. "You compare me too much to my daddy," she said. "I am my own horse and I want to be doing my own special thing. I want to do it my way and I want to have fun along the way." Her human told me that Felicity's father had won lots of competitions and she was training Felicity to do the same thing.

Felicity then showed me a picture of a badger who was her dear friend that she missed.

"That is amazing!" her human said. "I can't believe the horse told you about the badger." Felicity currently lived in a training facility in another state far from home and longed to be back with her friends.

Felicity told me these words and had me repeat them to her human: "I do not want to be an exact repeat of my daddy. I don't want to win the same things daddy wins. I want to do my own things. Please don't compare me to daddy." Then she showed me a picture of two large crystal trophies, which her human confirmed Felicity's sire had won.

Her human confessed that Felicity was really difficult to train and that her father was much easier. Felicity seemed irritated and said: "I want to do things my way and because I am being difficult she is learning lots of new things. If things were so easy breezy then she wouldn't be learning anything. You can't compare me to my daddy."

"Why did the apples stop?" Felicity demanded. "I would like to start having apples again."

Her human told me that the new trainer liked to give alfalfa treats instead of apples. She promised to call the trainer that afternoon to let her know that Felicity wanted apples instead of alfalfa.

Just like humans' animals do not necessarily like being compared to their parents.

Chapter 34: Stella the Cat

When I first communicated with Stella, she told me that she was having stomach issues. They had recently been to the vet because Stella had lost her appetite. Stella would be leaving her cat body soon to cross over the rainbow bridge.

Stella expressed she was here to teach her human lessons and to support her. They had learned a lot from each other. "She has blossomed and bloomed. Now she has a backbone," Stella said. Her human told me she understood the feeling exactly.

"My time is coming to leave this earth," Stella said. "But please know that I will still be around you. You don't need my support anymore. You were a little flower when I came into your life, and now you are a full bloom. When the day comes that you have to make a decision, please do not have any regrets. I want to spend this time with you by having you tell me everything that's on your mind. I have been your therapist for years, so I want to continue as your therapist because I am really good at it."

Stella wanted her human to remember the two of them playing with peacock feathers instead of how sad her passing would be. She would blink lights in her human's house after she passes to let her human know she was still present.

After Stella's passing, her human called to let me know that the lights *did* blink, just like Stella promised.

Sometimes the student-teacher roles can be reciprocal as Stella showed me.

Chapter 35: Lucky the Chesapeake Bay Retriever

When I met Lucky, he first communicated to me that he LOVES dock diving and that he lives for it. He felt that his human was not very invested this season because she was usually a very laidback person and seemed distracted at the competitions lately. Lucky's human admitted that she was nervous about him not doing as well at the upcoming event because of the pressure to win.

Lucky showed me a picture of orange cheese. "I love cheese!" he said. His human confirmed that she does give him orange cheese and that, yes, he does love it.

"Someone in the house snores loud…very loud!" Lucky said and showed me an image of himself shivering when he was trying to sleep the previous night. His human and her friend laughed because they were sharing a house and someone in one of the rooms *did* snore loudly. They also agreed that, for some odd reason, the rooms had been chilly.

Lucky showed me a picture of a tv and I heard him say, "It's on all night." His human laughed and said, yes, she often falls asleep with the tv on.

Lucky made sure to tell his human he was her bodyguard, and if there was ever danger he would kick someone's butt for her. "Tell her I would take a bullet for her. That is how much I love her," he said passionately. When I told his human, she became teary eyed and told me that this was exactly how she felt about him.

Lucky's human had a specific question she wanted to ask him, wanting to know what he thought of his dog sister. Lucky replied, "She is crazy and nuttier than a fruitcake. She isn't really related to me. I am much better than her. I picked up on all the tricks but she isn't able to as quickly." His human got quiet, laughed, then agreed.

As we got to the end of our session, Lucky wanted me to tell his human one of his wishes: "When we go for walks I like to stop and smell the roses and pee on things, but she doesn't allow me to do that. She is a fast walker and doesn't like to let me stop." His human told me that she would make an effort to walk slower and allow him more time to stop and smell.

Lucky knows the value of enjoying the journey as much as the destination.

Chapter 36: Scooby the American Staffordshire Terrier

I met with Scooby in person at a dog show event. When he walked in to see me, I could feel his energy: loving and confident.

"The judge was a female and she didn't have good vibes," he said. "No matter what I did, I wasn't going to impress her, so why waste my time?" His human told me they had just come out of the ring and she was frustrated because he didn't show well. She wondered if he didn't like to compete. Scooby communicated that he *does* like to show and wants to continue, but that he didn't want to waste his time when he knew he wasn't going to win.

Scooby communicated his human sometimes got a pain in her neck when they were showing and he could feel it in the leash. His human confirmed that this does happen once in a while when they are in the ring.

"We are two peas in a pod. And I am a rock star in this arena," he informed me. His human laughed because she also felt they were very close. And they were the current number one owner-handler pair in his breed, so she could see him giving himself the nickname.

Scooby then added that he and his human just had a photo taken together. His human said, "That is so weird you are saying this because we just took a photo over there just a few minutes ago. Wow, this is really strange!"

Scooby showed me a picture of a tooth being picked at by a human and requested that the water be a little warmer when his human bathed him. His human confirmed that she had been picking at one of his teeth, and she promised warmer water for him in the future.

"No one else looks like me," he added. I didn't quite understand what he meant, so I asked him to explain. He added: "My coloring is different from everyone else." When I told his human what he said to me, she validated that he was indeed unique and no one else in his breed class looked like him.

Scooby's human wanted to know what his favorite food was. When I asked him, he showed me a picture of something that looked like jerky and white meat. His human validated she had just given him a piece of jerky and white turkey meat earlier in the day.

As we were wrapping up our session, Scooby communicated to me that he wanted his human to be a better driver. "She likes to slam on the brakes," he said. His human confirmed that she did like to slam on the brakes and would take his advice and be a better driver.

In my book, Scooby is a ROCK STAR!

Chapter 37: Reno the Horse

When I first met with Reno, he showed me a picture of a horse halter and I saw the word "NEW" next to it. I asked his human if she had bought him a new halter, and she got quiet. She admitted she had just bought him a new halter, but there was no way he knew about it yet because she hadn't brought it to the barn yet.

"I have no idea how animals know the things they know," I said. "But I have had numerous animals tell me about things that their humans have said that they couldn't know about. But somehow they do know!"

Reno then showed me a picture of a horse bit labeled "not so new." When I asked his human what this could mean, she said she'd bought him a new bit around nine months back. So the "not so new" words made sense.

Then Reno showed me the image of a horse blanket and said, "I want a blankie." His human said she used to put a blanket on him, but hadn't lately because she hadn't thought he needed it. She promised to get it out again.

Reno told me that the farrier who comes to shoe the horses and trim their hooves is a "nut" and that the horses all talk about him. His human just laughed. She said she could see how he and the other horses might think of the farrier this way, but the humans thought he was excellent at his job.

Reno asked why he didn't have a stall with the "best view."

"Because half of his stall is blocked by a wall, and the other ones are more open," his human said.

"I am a really good horse and would like to have a room with a view," Reno insisted.

As our session came to a close, Reno showed me an outline of the state of Arizona. "She is going to this place," he said, so I asked his human if she was indeed going to Arizona.

Her mouth dropped and her response was: "Holy crap, how does he know that? I am not taking him with me but, yes, I am going to Arizona in the near future."

"You can't keep secrets from animals!"

Chapter 38: Emma the Horse

Emma's energy felt like she was shy and lacking confidence. Her human had rescued Emma from an auction and had appeared to be quite timid. Emma communicated to me that in her previous home she was not appreciated and her owners had neglected her.

"Is this my forever home?" Emma asked. Her human said she intended to keep Emma for the rest of her life.

I asked her human to do some homework for the next couple of weeks, suggesting she say to Emma "This is your forever home" out loud, a few times each day. In my experience with animals, they want to be assured they won't be rehomed. Once the animal truly trusts their human, they will begin to build a stronger bond.

Emma showed me a picture of a red fox and said, "This fox is my friend." Her human told me that there was a red fox who hung around the pasture and she had seen it several times. Her human couldn't believe Emma was talking about the fox and promised to watch out for it.

Emma showed me a picture of her walking over logs. I didn't understand the meaning of the picture, so I just explained the image to her human who said that they had been training this way for some time.

Emma loved her stall and pasture, then she showed me a picture of a big blue ball. "Best view," she said. Her human confirmed these details: her horse does have the best view and one of these balls.

Emma said she wouldn't mind getting her hair cut. Her human's mouth dropped open because she *had* been thinking about cutting Emma's mane and clipping her body fur, but hadn't expressed it out loud yet. She couldn't believe Emma had picked up on this.

As our session came to a close, Emma showed me a picture of what appeared to me to be rosary beads. Her human did not have rosary beads but she did have meditation beads. She asked me why Emma would show me a picture of those beads.

"She is showing me obscure objects to help prove to you that she is really communicating with me," I replied cheerfully.

Although Emma's energy felt like she was lacking confidence, she made it clear she knew what she had: a room with a view!

Chapter 39: Beau the Horse

B eau started off the conversation by saying, "Thank you! Thank you! Thank you for taking me away from the lady. She was dirty. I have gone from hoarders to the Taj Mahal." His human confirmed he had been found in filthy conditions with hoarders who did not take care of him properly. His human saved him, Beau said, but *he* had also saved *her*.

Beau didn't want his human to focus on the "hoarders" part of his life and instead wanted her to focus on the here and now. He said he hadn't reached his full potential yet and was going to be a king, not a prince. I got chills when he told me his truth.

Beau insisted he could do "tricks." His human confirmed she was teaching him to bow and other complicated dressage moves.

I couldn't help but laugh at the next picture Beau showed me during our session: a yellow rubber chicken. His human chuckled and told me about a video of a horse flinging a yellow rubber duck on the internet which she had just posted to her Facebook page.

"How could he possibly know about a video I watched. I didn't show it to him. Do you think he wants a rubber chicken?" she asked.

I laughed so hard my stomach ached and told her she may want to look into getting him a chicken since he was showing me a picture of it.

Beau didn't want his human to be mad at him about his really smelly gas. His human confirmed this and agreed she wouldn't get mad at him about it. Beau showed me a picture of apples and peanut butter. His human confirmed he liked apples, but she didn't know about the peanut butter.

Beau's human wanted to know what he thought of the equipment she had for him. He showed me a picture of a plaid pad. "Like thick," Beau said. His human promised to use the thicker pad more often.

"Reins smell," Beau added. I didn't know what this meant, so his human explained that she had just cleaned his reins and, yes, they did smell different. He also added, "Kings don't wear bows." His human admitted she had put a bow on him for Christmas and had taken a picture which she posted to Facebook. She had thought maybe he hadn't liked the bow. As she spoke about the bow I got chills!

I then felt Beau's energy change to a much more serious attitude. "I don't want her to put anything silly on Facebook about me. I am a king and I don't want to be like Kim Kardashian and have zillions of pictures out there of me," Beau said.

His human told me she takes pictures of him all the time and posts them online. She promised not to put up silly pictures of him or dress him up with bows anymore.

This horse was a most dignified and kingly presence. No more bows for Beau!

Chapter 40: Murphy the Horse

Murphy started our session by showing me the number five. His human told me she has had him for five years, so this number made sense.

The energy I felt from Murphy was very sassy and funny. "I am just like her, I am OCD just like her" he said, smiling. His human chuckled and acknowledged that she is very OCD and yes he seems to be like that as well. As I stated previously animals are a reflection of their humans so it would make sense why he would act similarly.

Murphy told me he wanted to address the change in his food. "Cheap food. Yuck!" he exclaimed. His food had been changed to a cheaper brand, his human confessed, because she was trying to save money.

Murphy showed me a picture of a room full of ribbons he had earned and proudly showed me a trophy cup. "Awesome!" Murphy repeated over and over. I could feel the pride radiating off of Murphy as he recounted his accomplishments.

Murphy showed me a picture of his front left hoof which appeared to be wrapped up. Then he said "annoying" and showed me an image of the hoof unwrapped. His human confirmed that he'd torn a tendon, and it kept coming unwrapped. She could definitely see how he would think it was annoying!

Murphy said he did *not* want glitter on him. His human had done this to another horse but not to him and he wanted to make sure she knew how he felt before putting it on him. (Hold the glitter, human!)

Murphy showed me a picture of his teeth and a very large toothpick. His human laughed when I described what he was showing me because his teeth had just been looked at by the vet.

The last thing Murphy wished for was warmer bath water. The last time she had given him a bath, the shampoo she used smelled "girly" to him. His human laughed and promised to change the shampoo back to the old brand and to warm up the water.

Murphy was one opinionated fellow!

Chapter 41: George the Horse

I had the pleasure of chatting with a 30-year-old horse named George who told me immediately: "I am not old. I am still a spring chicken." He wanted me to know that he is *very* smart because he can turn knobs, and his human confirmed these details.

"I am a big boy. I am *not* fat," the horse said. (At sixteen hands, he *is* quite tall for a horse.)

He started talking about the "little dog" who is his friend and how he likes it when people talk to him or play music around him. He showed me an image of his head bobbing up and down to the beat.

The last thing George communicated before our session ended was that he hears the song "Let It Go" (from the movie *Frozen*) too often. He asked if his human would play a different song. His exact words were: "Can you tell her to *let go* of the 'Let It Go' song. It drives me nuts." His human promised to find some new songs to play for him.

A little variety in music can go a long way!

Chapter 42: Ted the Turtle

Ted has lived with his human for the past twenty-five years and he *adores* his human. His human told me she adores him as well. He especially loves when she rubs his belly and legs. He showed me a picture of a bottle of body oil/lotion.

"He is showing me body oil or lotion. Do you put body oil him?" I asked his human. This was a new one for me, so I felt kind of odd asking, but at the same time I was curious to find out the meaning of this image.

His human smiled and nodded. "Yes, I do. Does he like it?"

"I *love* it!" Ted replied.

I asked what type of oil she used because I had never heard of a special turtle oil before. She laughed and said it was called "Wesson Oil" which kept his skin from cracking.

"I love it!" Ted repeated. He smiled at his human often and wanted to make sure she knew what the gesture meant.

"Yes! He *does* smile," she said, astonished.

Before the end of our session, Ted asked me to tell his human again that he really loves her and the massages.

Who knew turtles loved oil massages?

Chapter 43: Roscoe the Black Lab

Roscoe's most important concern was the tile floor in the house. He showed me an image of fingers on a chalkboard and said: "Don't like tile floor. It feels like chalk."

His human had noticed his reluctance to walk on the tile floor and was wondering why he didn't like it. Now everything made sense! He didn't like how the floor felt on his feet or the rough texture. His human promised not to try to coax him onto the floor now that she knew how he felt about it.

Roscoe then showed me a picture of a man sitting in a recliner along with the words "snores loudly." His human laughed because this man was her husband. She said sometimes Roscoe would even leave the room if the sound got too loud and had wondered if it bothered him.

His human was curious to know which of his toys was his favorite: the pig or the duck. Roscoe showed me the duck.

In closing, Roscoe asked for warm water on his evening meal. He got up several times during the night and explained that the water would help fill his belly so he wouldn't have to get up so much. His human said she would definitely do this in the future.

It's usually the human complaining about a snoring dog, but here's an example of the very opposite!

Chapter 44: Geraldine the Lhasa Apso

I communicated with Geraldine after she passed. The first thing she showed me was the rainbow bridge, though it was different than I had seen before, with brighter colors and wider lines.

"I crossed the rainbow bridge, and it was a huge celebration," Geraldine said.

I asked her to show me who greeted her on the other side because her human wanted to know who was there.

"Saint Francis of Assisi walked with me across the bridge," she replied.

I couldn't believe what Geraldine showed me next: Mother Teresa with a huge smile on her face, Noah's Ark, and a string of rosary beads.

"I have never seen anything like this before with such intensity. Are you a religious person?" I asked Geraldine's human.

"Yes," she said quickly, then asked me to tell her more about what I saw.

Geraldine insisted again that her passing was a huge celebration. Many people had lined up on the bridge when she crossed over, including religious figures from the Catholic faith like popes, nuns, and cardinals from the past. I had grown up Catholic, so I was able to understand who they were. I told her human what I was seeing, but she didn't comment. She just smiled and asked what else Geraldine was communicating. All the people Geraldine showed me had smiles on their faces, and I could feel the joy and love radiating from them.

Geraldine showed me the numbers 8 and 26.

"Do you understand these numbers?" I asked. "Was Geraldine 8 years old when she passed? Or did she pass on the 26th day of the month?"

"No," her human replied. "The numbers don't mean anything to me."

But the numbers had some special meaning to Geraldine, so I kept them in mind. At a later time, the meaning might become clearer.

Geraldine then communicated that she did not want her "mommy" to have any guilt for not being there when she died. Geraldine had passed in her sleep painlessly, and there was nothing her human could have done to save her life. "I want mommy to remember all the fun times we had and not focus on the final moment of my life. The final moment is not who I am. I am full of joy and laughter and want her to remember that."

As our session came to a close, Geraldine added, "Tell my mommy I love her and that I will always be around her. Let her know I am in heaven. Animals really do have souls and go to heaven."

After our session, I visited with Geraldine's human for a time because what I had seen seemed so miraculous and vivid. Her human was indeed a religious person and she religiously practiced her Catholic faith. She had been praying to Saint Francis of Assisi, the Patron Saint of Animals, to meet Geraldine at the rainbow bridge. She had been absent when Geraldine passed and had a lot of guilt about it.

When I asked her if she understood why Geraldine would show me Mother Teresa, she explained to me that Geraldine passed on September 4th which was the same day Mother Teresa was declared a saint by the Catholic Church. Just as she was telling me this, I got goosebumps all over me. Now I understood the "huge celebration" piece of Geraldine's story. Not only was it the day of her passing but, amazingly enough, it had also been a huge day in the spirit world for Mother Teresa.

Geraldine's human then told me that her son was a priest and that he had known about the session. Both of them hoped Geraldine had made it safely through her passing and was happy on the other side. Her son had said: "Mom, I truly believe animals have souls, that they go to heaven, and that we will see them again."

I realized Geraldine had validated his belief about animals having souls and going to heaven. Amazing!

A few days after our session, Geraldine's human called to update me. She and her son spoke about our session and he had been amazed, especially the part about animals having souls and going to heaven. She still couldn't figure out the significance of the numbers, but her son had some ideas.

"Mom those numbers are the birthdate of Mother Teresa," her son said. "August 26. And don't you remember Geraldine was born on the same date? You specifically adopted Geraldine because of her birthdate." I got goosebumps as she shared this information!

When I got off the phone with Geraldine's human, I was in awe at all the information Geraldine shared with us. I always say that Animals Are Amazing, and Geraldine did an exceptional job of showing us just how amazing she is.

Chapter 45: Heidi the Maltese

When I first sat down with Heidi and her human, I was surprised at what I was hearing. Right off the bat, Heidi wanted to show me her humorous side.

"Heidi Heidi Heidi Ho," the dog sang.

I relayed this to her human and she started to laugh. "That's exactly what I sing to her!"

Heidi showed me a picture of a pink blanket, and I kept hearing: "Very soft, very soft. Cashmere." Her human confirmed Heidi did have a pink cashmere blanket and it was very soft. I was stunned because this was the first animal I had ever chatted with who had a cashmere blanket and knew exactly what it was made out of.

Heidi told me she did *not* like bows in her hair when she went to the groomer. Her human promised she would make sure they didn't use bows anymore.

Heidi wondered why her treats had been cut down and said, "I am *not* fat." Her human had indeed cut down on treats because of Heidi's weight.

Heidi then showed me her teeth. I asked if her human was picking at her teeth or cleaning her teeth a lot, but she shook her head no. Again, Heidi showed me her teeth. Her human told me she had recently gone to the vet and was told she had an infection in her teeth and would have to get some of them pulled. I got goosebumps as she spoke.

Lastly, Heidi told me about the first time they had met, saying it was "love at first sight." Her human responded by saying "It was love at first sight when I met Heidi." I could see the bond between them and the happiness they shared.

Chapter 46: Sherlock the English Labrador

I met Sherlock at a dock diving competition, and the first thing he wanted to tell me was he *loved* this sport and he was *very* good at it.

During our session, I couldn't get the image of a red vest out of my mind, so I asked his human if he had one but she said he didn't. Again, he showed me a vest, only this time it was the color orange. His human seemed baffled, having no idea what this was about. Sherlock showed me the picture three more times.

I turned to his human and said, "I don't know why he's stuck on these vests, but maybe you will understand it in the future. Sometimes animals show me what they want or what's going to happen in the future."

Sherlock went on to tell me that he was excellent with his nose. "I am *really* good at my sniffing abilities," he repeated over and over. I then asked his human to explain what he may mean by that, and she told me that he was a cadaver dog, therefore his nose work had to be really sensitive to find dead bodies.

Just before our session ended Sherlock told me that 2019 was going to be an "Explosive Year" for the two of them. His human didn't really know what this meant, and neither did I, but I felt like something good was coming for the two of them.

The next day, Sherlock and his human stopped by my booth to say hello and to show me something very significant.

"Look at what he is wearing today. You told me yesterday he was showing you a red and an orange vest and I kept telling you that he did not have one." his human said with a grin.

"Oh, wow! Did you just buy him the vest?" I asked, noting the red and orange on it. "Did you get this particular one because I told you the colors red and orange?"

"No!" she replied. "I would have bought something blue or green, but this was the only one they had in his size."

Sherlock must have known the vest was coming!

I followed up with Sherlock's human after our session to see if the "Explosive Year" comment meant anything yet. She told me when they had returned home from the show, she got a call from her town's police department asking if they could put Sherlock on the list of rescue police force for *explosives*.

I could barely believe my ears! Sherlock knows a *lot* more than we humans do!

Chapter 47: Jasmine the Yorkie

The first words Jasmine said to me were: "I am the Princess. I am the Princess." Her human agreed with Jasmine's statement as she told me they do call her "Princess" sometimes.

Jasmine communicated she doesn't walk like a regular dog: she prances. I got an image of the dog prancing on wood and tile floor, and I kept hearing "click, click, click" in my head. Jasmine *loved* this sound because it told people she was coming. Then I saw a scene of brass trumpets being blown like a court announcing a queen. Her human agreed that Jasmine *does* prance across the flooring and that she thought the yorkie enjoyed making noise.

"I hate to be cold," Jasmine informed me, showing me an image of herself under the covers and with an electric blanket. Her human explained that Jasmine has her very own knit blanket to cuddle.

"I do *not* like the snow," Jasmine added, showing me a scene of herself going potty in the snow. "It's to freaking cold outside and I don't like how snow feels on my feet."

"It's funny she mentions cold weather, because we live in the warm part of the country. But we just went to a cold area where it snows," her human said. "She did seem to hate it!"

Jasmine communicated she may be a little dog, but she can go from 0 to zooming in two seconds. "I'm super-fast!" she said.

Her human laughed and agreed. As her human validated the statement, I got goosebumps.

Jasmine said she was meant to be with her human. The Yorkie was originally supposed to go to someone else, but the adoption had fallen through. When her human saw her picture, she had fallen in love with Jasmine instantly.

Jasmine said "a grandmother in spirit who loved animals and who adores her human" had sent her to her human. I asked the human if this made sense, and she told me that her grandmother, who loved dogs and whom she had a special connection with, had passed when she was a teenager.

Her human added: "You know it is kind of weird because, since I have gotten Jasmine, I have had vivid dreams of my grandmother." As she was saying these words to me I again got goosebumps all over.

The picture of Jasmine that I held during our session was one of her wearing a red dog dress. It was one of Jasmine's favorites because she looked so cute in it. She said: "Mommy needs a little girl to dress up in frilly stuff. She needs me because I am the frilly girl in her life." Her human confirmed that she has daughters who didn't enjoy "frilly stuff" like Jasmine does.

Jasmine showed me a picture of a sweater with a fur collar, which her human confirmed.

"It's funny to have an extra fur coat when you have your own fur," I laughed.

"I have all this beauty inside and out," Jasmine said, showing me a picture of her visiting the senior citizens, "and I should be sharing it with people. I would be a big hit at a senior home because they would appreciate my beauty and my outfits."

Jasmine informed me she wanted to be a therapy dog and visit senior citizens at the local nursing home. Her human didn't have any plans to do therapy work now, but Jasmine wanted her to know she would be interested in doing that line of work in the future.

"But don't put those booties or the harness on me again," the Yorkie added. The last harness had chafed and been very uncomfortable. Her human promised to find one Jasmine might like better.

Jasmine loved her new white bowl, saying, "It is beautiful." Her human said the new cute bowl had been a Christmas present.

The yorkie showed me little pencil eraser-sized treats saying, "I don't get these anymore." Her human had stopped giving them to her because she was having some tummy issues.

Jasmine then showed me bananas and pineapples, and her human said she eats bananas and shares them with Jasmine but hadn't in a couple of weeks. I thought the pineapples were odd, but her human laughed and told me she did indeed give her little pieces of pineapple every once in a while.

As I was looking at Jasmine's picture, I silently told her that she had an adorable face and I heard her say, "Yes, this face needs to be in a calendar. She should make a calendar of me." When I told her human what she said, she laughed. She said she took pictures of Sophie all the time and Jasmine seemed to love posing!

Jasmine liked music, but she doesn't like "the crazy music" as she called it. Her human mostly listened to Christian music; her daughter and her husband are the ones who listen to the rap and pop music the Yorkie didn't appreciate.

As our session wrapped up, Jasmine's human told me she used to work as a home healthcare nurse with mostly senior citizen clients. She always joked with her husband that maybe she should go back to work and bring Jasmine with her.

I got goosebumps for a third time! It was no coincidence that Jasmine kept talking about going to visit seniors during our session and that her human had been having these conversations. Jasmine gave her approval for her human to work with the elderly and take her along!

Chapter 48: Sophie the Dog

When I started our session, I didn't recognize what breed Sophie was, so I asked. Sophie responded: "In the animal world it doesn't matter what breed you are. I am a dog. You humans are all concerned about what color you are, and it really doesn't matter you are all humans. We are all animals, and it doesn't matter if you are a dachshund, a lab, or a boxer. Who cares? You humans are so hung up on classifying things."

I thought this was an astute observation from a very smart dog!

Sophie said she really helped her human, though she wasn't a trained therapy dog. Her human agreed Sophie had provided a lot of emotional support to her.

Sophie showed me a picture of a rainbow pile of dog clothes. I asked her human if she bought her clothes, and then I asked Sophie if she liked them. Her human confirmed she bought her clothes.

"Yes, sometimes I liked the clothes, and then sometimes I would think what the freak was she thinking?" Sophie replied. I couldn't help but laugh at her funny response.

Sophie said her human daddy wasn't happy at first when she had arrived, but she eventually got him wrapped around her paw. Sophie's human had gotten the dog as a surprise for her husband and the moment she saw Sophie it was love at first sight. Her friend had encouraged her to look at another dog, but she wouldn't because she knew instantly Sophie was "the one."

Sophie, who had recently passed, had crossed the rainbow bridge and was perfect and whole once again. She showed me a picture of rosary beads and told me she had been greeted by St. Francis of Assisi, the Patron Saint of Animals on the other side. Sophie's human was not religious but her husband was, so these symbols would make sense to him. She insisted I tell her human that her passing was peaceful.

Sophie emphasized she had been the princess of the house and asserted that the other dog in the house was "Bozo the Clown." Her human laughed, saying she could envision Sophie saying this. Sophie told me she had her own special blanket and her human had given it to another animal to use. She was a little perturbed her blanket had been given away, but she didn't mind the new dog using her old toys.

At this point Sophie's human pulled out a photograph of another dog sitting on Sophie's blanket. Immediately, Sophie scoffed that this was the "clown" she didn't like using her blanket. According to her human, Sophie had never met this dog because she had already passed by the time they had adopted the new dog. I explained gently that Sophie knows about this dog because she is able to see what is going on even in her spirit form.

"The candle is for me," Sophie said. Her human explained she *had* lit a candle in front of Sophie's picture at her wedding in her honor. This gave me chills!

I saw an image of Sophie pressed up against the back of her human's legs, which was how she used to snuggle with her human when she was alive.

Sophie showed me an image of two red cardinals in a backyard and said: "I am sending the one cardinal and a father is sending the other one." When I asked her human if her father was deceased, she said no and that he was standing right beside her. I then asked her father if *his* father was deceased and he said "yes" and then I got goosebumps. Sophie's human said they see cardinals sometimes but not very often. She promised to keep her eyes open for them.

Sophie showed me a picture of herself sleeping on a pillow under the covers. Her human confirmed Sophie did like to sleep in the bed and on the pillows and under the covers. Sophie added she liked to go under the bed for "alone time," but her human said they didn't have a bed she could crawl under. The dog cleared this up by showing me a vision of a futon, which her human said they did have.

Then I saw an image of Sophie sitting on the back of the couch like a cat. Even though her human said she wasn't allowed to sit up there, Sophie kept showing me the picture. After a minute or two, her human said the dogs got in trouble for sitting up there. As she told me this I got goosebumps!

"Bingo!" said Sophie, laughing and shaking her head up and down.

Apparently, Sophie *did* sit on the back of the couch, but only when her human wasn't around because she knew she would get into trouble.

Sophie showed me a picture of a mouse, so I asked her human if she had ever caught a mouse and brought it to her. Her human said she couldn't remember her catching a mouse. Sophie showed me the mouse several more times.

"We have chinchillas and they sort of look like big mice," her human said.

"That must be it because I got goosebumps!"

I then asked if she knew why Sophie would be showing me the mouse, and her human told me that Sophie enjoyed playing with the chinchillas. The dog was showing me a happy time in her life, wanting her human to remember the happy times instead of the day of her passing.

Chapter 49: Basil the Horse

Basil communicated she *loves* her name. Her human told me she had just gotten her five months ago and changed the horse's name to Basil when she arrived.

The horse showed me the number seven, but it did not make sense to me or her human at first. Apparently, Basil was at auction in a group of ten horses, of which she was the seventh, so this number was important to her.

Then Basil said her human was not consistent in her training; she was "wishy-washy and couldn't make up her mind." Her human agreed, explaining that Basil was her first horse so she had started from scratch.

"Sometimes I can't decide what we should work on for the day and wonder if we worked too much on a single task. I question myself a lot," her human said.

Basil wanted me to ask her human if she was going to keep her. Her human responded by telling me Basil was not going anywhere, she was keeping Basil until the end. Basil communicated she knew it had been hard for her human to buy her at auction.

Her human said: "Yes, it was a struggle to convince the person to sell me the horse. My friend helped convince them." I got goosebumps as she was confirming what Basil communicated.

Basil informed me that she was a very special horse. Her human said she was bred very well from a very good bloodline. The horse then showed me a picture of her teeth, so I asked her human if there was something going on with her teeth.

"Basil is teething right now," her human replied. "She's losing some of her baby teeth."

"Is she getting a new pad and saddle?" I asked on Basil's behalf. She informed me she *did not* want someone's hand-me-downs saying "I do not want dirty stuff. I am a princess!"

Her human *was* going to buy her a new saddle, but had been waiting until she was fully grown. She had just bought a used saddle pad, and Basil wanted to know if it had been washed. Her human said she had not washed it yet but would wash it soon.

Basil then showed me an image of a dog doing agility by jumping over a stick, so I asked if horses did agility like dogs. Her human said she and Basil were starting to work with obstacles where she had to learn to pick up her feet over a jump. Basil also showed me a picture of herself walking backwards holding a rope. Her human validated this was part of the training and I got goosebumps!

Basil said she is "really brain smart like Einstein." Her human agreed that her bloodline is bred for a really good brain, bone structure, and hooves. The horse knew she would be competing in the upcoming year, and her human would be taking her back to the barn where she was auctioned to attend the event.

Basil showed me the words "doctor cancel," three times. I asked her human: "Did you cancel a doctor appointment?"

"No," she said, baffled. "I didn't."

"No! *She* cancelled a doctor appointment. She needs to go to the doctor," Basil repeated.

Basil's human immediately turned to her mother and said, "How many times have I told you: you need to go to the doctor to get a checkup?" I got goosebumps as she was talking to her mother.

I turned to the woman's mother and said "This is the horse telling you this because I do not know you. So maybe you don't listen to your daughter, but maybe you should listen to the horse. It must be something very important if she brought it up repeatedly."

"Alright, I will listen to you and Basil and go to the doctor," she agreed finally.

"See I am so much more than just a horse," Basil said.

There is something to be said about horse sense!

Chapter 50: Ricardo the Horse

When I looked at Ricardo's picture, I felt a humorous spirit coming from him. He was acting really goofy in the picture and his human said his silliness always made her smile.

I asked his human what breed of horse he was and she said he was "a grey," which is not a breed but a color. I have to admit that I am not up to speed on horse breeds and had thought he was a donkey at first.

"Lady, you need to get a horse dictionary because you don't know breeds," Ricardo said in response to me asking his human his breed.

I communicated with Ricardo in spirit form because his human had to make the decision to release him to the other side.

"I had cancer, and it was all in me," Ricardo said. "It just wasn't in one place; it was all over me."

I then heard the song "I Did It My Way" by Frank Sinatra in my head. Ricardo told me to tell his human: "Even though you had to make the decision, I left this world my way. This was my way of going out. I didn't break a leg; it was all internal." I got goosebumps as I told his human what he said, so I knew this was something very important he wanted her to know. Ricardo showed me four people around him when it came time for him to depart this world. His human validated this number.

Ricardo wanted me to know he was "really fast" and his human agreed, saying he always outran the other horses. He then showed me a picture of his one foot going out to the side when he was running. I didn't understand what this meant but then I heard the words "trot and canter." I told his human what I was seeing and hearing, then asked if this made sense. His human confirmed during his gait transitions he would stick one foot out in an odd way just for a second between trot and canter.

I then saw an image of what appeared to be a horse digging a hole, and his human said he would often paw at the ground. I was shown a picture of 2 grumpy old men and asked her if she knew what this could mean. His human had retired him when he'd gotten older and gave the horse to her dad.

"Yeah, two grumpy old men need to be together," Ricardo said, then added: "I love the sun, but she was always worried I'd get sunburned."

His human had worried about this because he was a grey with light skin and fur. Ricardo snorted: "What are you talking about? I am a horse! I don't get sunburned." He said he hated the smell of suntan lotion and his fly mask. (On a side note I have since found out that horses are able to get sunburned.)

Ricardo showed me a chunk of his hair and said his human was unsure what to do with it. "Tell her to make a bracelet out of it," he insisted.

"My eyelashes were beautiful compared to other horses," Ricardo said, showing me an image of them. His human agreed that he did have long, beautiful lashes.

In closing, Ricardo said, "Please tell her there was nothing she could have done to prevent my passing. And I don't want her to feel any guilt." He had passed on a sunny, warm day, and his human confirmed it had been a beautiful day.

Ricardo had a distinct smell and said that his human has smelled him since his passing. She quietly confirmed this, seeming a bit sad for a moment.

"When you see him in a very vivid dream or if you think you smell him: this is real," I told her. "Do not discredit visits from the spirit world. It is a gift."

Chapter 51: Ford the Horse

I met Ford in person and the first thing I heard from Ford was, "Ask her if she has changed my name yet." He wanted a more regal-sounding name because he felt he was a king, a name fit for a king like George or Henry. His human said she had not changed his name yet, but had thought about it and would make an effort to come up with a new name.

Ford said his human had gotten him at a "hell of a good price," and I kept hearing the words "short sale." The people she had purchased him from came down in price three times, so she had gotten him cheaply. I got goosebumps when his human confirmed what Ford told me.

"Thoroughbreds get a bad rap," Ford said. "People think they are destined to run and run and run, but I like to slow down, eat grass, and smell the roses. Don't listen to all those stereotypes. Ask her what she wants to do with me. I don't know what my purpose is. I don't know what she wants to do with me."

His human wanted to jump with him, but was nervous about it because he likes to stop and look at things.

"Oh, he said he likes to stop and smell the roses sometimes," I replied. "No need to be afraid." I got goosebumps when I said the words "No need to be afraid".

Then Ford wanted to know if he and his human would be doing some special training, adding "We need to do some groundwork." His human confirmed both of these things to be true. I got the chills!

Ford said he wanted to build a better bond with his human because he knew his human was considering not keeping him. When I asked her if this was true, she admitted that she wasn't sure it was the right fit. Ford requested they stand outside by a tree together and have a heart to heart talk so he would know what exactly she wanted from him.

The horse then showed me a picture of himself wearing a sweater. I laughed and said: "I don't think horses wear sweaters, but I see him wearing one. Does this make sense to you?"

She had just bought him a blanket the previous week and had put it on him. I believe Ford was putting some humor into the conversation by showing me a horse in a sweater.

Ford told me he liked his food much better than what he'd eaten before. He showed me a picture of a food bowl with something on top of the grain, but I couldn't decipher what it was.

"Do you put something on his food?" I asked his human.

I got goosebumps when his human said, "Oh yeah, sometimes sunflower seeds."

"I like what she puts on my food," Ford said, showing me an image of him licking his lips. "I like warm water instead of cold, and I would like to have my water bowl cleaned more often." His human said she would take note of this.

Ford said he didn't have a saddle that fit him properly and needed a new one. His human explained he had lost some weight and she was waiting for him to gain it back before she bought a new one.

"When you get the new saddle, please get a second opinion," Ford said. "My saddle needs to fit me well if we are going to be jumping." Again, his human promised to take note of what he said.

Finally, Ford wanted me to ask his human this question: "Are you wanting to go to the International?" I had no idea what it meant, but asked it anyway and his human appeared to know exactly what he meant.

"Yes, I would like to," she replied, nodding vigorously.

"We are going. We are going. I will take you there," Ford said with enthusiasm. His human had a huge smile on her face when he communicated these words. I got the chills!

Everyone needs a goal to pursue, even a horse!

Chapter 52: Johnny the Horse

Right off the bat, Johnny's human wanted to know if the horse liked riding in the indoor riding ring.

"No," Johnny replied. He showed me the picture of himself running through nature off the beaten path. "Going around and around in circles is boring. I want to go outside."

Johnny then showed me the number 6 and said: "Ask her what was going on with my food during the past 6 weeks. I am not getting full and I am not fat!" His human had changed his food and cut it back a little because he had been gaining weight. She promised to look into a better solution for his food.

Johnny said he was going to have some footwork done, and his human confirmed an upcoming farrier appointment. He then showed me a picture of horseshoes and a piece of foam in one of them. His human nodded in agreement because he did have a wedge in one of his shoes.

Johnny saw himself as a "gentle giant," and his human called him a good boy who is "ruggedly handsome."

"Of course, I am handsome," the horse said. "I am Johnny Cash and I command respect and I get respect from the other horses."

I had just spoken to another horse about getting a blanket for the season and asked if Johnny wanted one. He said he did, but his human shook her head and said, "No he isn't getting a blanket. He has plenty of thick fur."

When I was chatting with Johnny, there were a few other people around listening. After hearing his human's response to the blanket, Johnny physically turned his head around and looked straight at his human. The expression on Johnny's face was priceless because, even if you don't communicate with animals like I do, you could see his look of disgust!

I suggested to his human she may want to look into getting a blanket for him because of his reaction to her response. This horse knows what he wants!

Chapter 53: Sunny the Dog

When I communicated with Sunny, she had already crossed over the rainbow bridge. "I love my mommy," she said. Her human addressed herself as "mommy" to Sunny because she felt such a maternal tie to her.

After asking what breed Sunny was, she responded: "I am a jack of all trades. I am a combination of a whole lot of dogs. I could have even come from Italy because I have so many different bloodlines running through me."

I turned to her human and asked if there was a strong connection with Italy because I felt there was a reason Sunny had mentioned this specific one and not another country.

"My father was in the war in Italy and I am named after my dad's girlfriend in the war," said her human. "We have a lot of pictures of Italy."

I got goosebumps when she told me this. Sunny was letting us know that she knew about the significance of the country to her human. She could have said any country in the world, but she chose Italy and I truly believe there are no coincidences.

"I love scrambled eggs and cheese. I am *not* fat," Sunny said. Her human agreed because Sunny did love this dish and laughed. Sunny had a few extra pounds but was not obese.

Sunny showed me an image of a toy and I kept hearing the words, "I did *not* un-stuff my toy. I did *not* un-stuff my toy." She'd had a pink monkey for a long time that did not have stuffing in it, her human said, so she had not "un-stuffed" it. But if her toys were stuffed, Sunny would take them apart.

Sunny wanted me to thank her human for releasing her to the other side, then showed me a picture of her ashes. Sunny had been cremated and her ashes were in the house, which her human confirmed. Sunny then communicated to me that she had been gone for some time and recently there had been talk about what to do with her ashes. Her human couldn't believe Sunny knew about this conversation. I told her Sunny knew about the conversation because she was right there in spirit form when the discussion took place.

Sunny showed me the number 2 and, when I asked her human if she had gotten her at two-years-old, she told me that she had gotten her when she was 2 months old in the month of February. Knowing the significance gave me chills!

Sunny then showed me the oddest picture: a child and a dog in what looked like a basket being pushed down a hill. I told her human what I was seeing and asked if this made any sense to her. Her human didn't know what it meant, but then her daughter spoke up. When she was younger, the older sister had put her and the dog in a laundry basket and pushed them down the stairs. *Ouch!* Sunny's human was surprised to hear this because she hadn't known about it either.

Then her human had me ask Sunny what had happened to her bowl after she passed. Sunny said she had broken the bowl because she didn't want anyone else to use it.

Her human had found the broken, ceramic bowl after coming home from the vet after releasing Sunny to the other side. She hadn't been able to figure out what had happened to it because it hadn't fallen off of anything. Sunny let her human know she could do amazing things in spirit form!

Chapter 54: A Horse Named Houdini

When I looked at Houdini's picture, I felt lots of confidence and humor radiating off of him in waves. He did not disappoint me during our session, starting off by telling me that he was "super smart, super smart!"

I then saw him moving his head up and down, and he told me he knows how to get out of "difficult situations." I didn't understand what he meant exactly, so I asked his human. She laughed and said this made total sense to her because they'd had to "horse proof" the barn because he could open doors and locks.

"You know those escape rooms you humans do? I can do them with no problem," Houdini said laughing.

Now I personally have never seen a horse in an escape room, but I didn't doubt he could do it after hearing from Houdini and his human.

Houdini added he liked music but complained that the music in the barn "goes fuzzy and needs to be fixed." His human told me there is a boom box in the barn and she would look to see if the station needed to be tuned.

Who knew horses could be magicians?

Chapter 55: Brucie the Rottweiler

I met Brucie in person with his human and a couple of her friends. When Brucie first sat down, I don't think he really believed I could communicate with him because I heard him say, "Well, this is going to be interesting."

"I hope so, because here is your opportunity to let your human know what's on your mind," I replied.

Brucie then lifted his head up and looked straight at me. "Oh, wow, you can really hear me?"

"Yes, I can."

I could feel Brucie's energy become lighter and more joyous once he knew I could hear him. He told me he loved his human and how she laughed, saying it was "funny." His human didn't really understand what he meant by this, but her friends agreed with Brucie.

Brucie also loved his human's friends and insisted he was a happy dog with no complaints except for one. The picture Brucie showed me made my jaw drop: a Chucky doll.

I am not a big fan of scary movies and when I saw this I got a bit nervous. But Brucie encouraged me to ask about the doll.

I turned to his human and asked: "This is really odd, but do you have a Chucky doll? Because your dog is showing me a picture of one."

She started laughing and so did her friends. "Yes, as a matter of fact I do have a Chucky doll."

"Ask her why she has a Chucky doll," said Brucie.

She responded that she loved the film and had recently bought a doll from the movie.

"Tell her I HATE IT," Brucie replied.

When I relayed this information, she seemed surprised. The doll was currently on the floor in a room Brucie frequented, and she promised to move it so he didn't have to see it.

"Who the hell has a Chucky doll?" Brucie exclaimed.

"I can honestly say I haven't known anyone, up until now," I replied.

Brucie repeated, "Tell her I hate it."

Then I was shown the word "IT" in all caps and the word kept getting bigger and bolder. His human explained her obsession with Stephen King movies. She loved the movie IT and had recently watched the film as well. I got goosebumps as she told me about the movie.

"I don't like that scary shit," Brucie said bluntly.

After a lot of laughter from his human and her friends, she said she would make sure he wasn't around when she watched scary movies anymore.

It turns out animals do understand what we watch and have their own tastes. I agree with Brucie!

Chapter 56: Millie the Horse

I met Millie in person and, when we started communicating, she said someone had beaten her with a stick or a whip. Her human nodded, saying they knew Millie had been abused in her previous home.

The horse communicated to me there is a certain type of movement people do which makes her think she is going to be beaten. She did not tell me specifically what the movement was, but her human confirmed what Millie was saying and the hair stood up on my arms.

"Where I came from, there was a lot of yelling and intimidation," Millie said. "They tried to 'break' me. It was a dirty, hoarding place."

Her human nodded because she had been told this by others who were familiar with the farm where her horse had lived. Millie declared that she was *done* talking about the past and had already explained all of these details to her human. She wanted to talk about the present instead.

"I am not a princess, but a queen," Millie said. "I have a really good home, but I would like a softer bed."

Her human laughed and pointed out that Millie already lives in a stall with deep bedding.

"I am putting in all my requests now," Millie said resolutely. "I might as well since the animal communicator can hear me."

The horse insisted that someone was not cleaning out her stall well enough. They didn't find all of her poop and needed to do a better job, though she didn't want to throw anyone under the bus. This was the reason she was asking for more bedding because queens do not lie in their poop and pee.

Her human hadn't been out riding lately, and the horse wanted to know the reason. Millie had some really bad arthritis in her legs because of where she came from and how the previous people treated her, so her human didn't want to injure her.

Millie then showed me a picture of her human on a horse with Millie tied next to the other horse. I asked her human if this was something she had done with Millie, but she said no, they hadn't. She said they could try it in the future so they could both get some fresh air. Millie nodded her head up and down, enthusiastically agreeing with her human.

The horse didn't want her human to feel sorry for her or be so tender with her because the terrible part of life was over now. "Now let's go have fun," Millie said.

Her human did feel badly about what happened to Millie and didn't know how to make up for it.

"If she wants to make up for it, then take me outside and take me for a ride. Let's go have some fun and not be sad," Millie communicated to me. "You cannot fix what happened in the past. And if I didn't have all the bad things happen to me in the past, then I probably wouldn't be here with her. So, I had to go through it to get to her now." I got the chills as Millie was communicating.

Millie, who was very wise, continued to offer her opinion: "Do you think your Grandma would want you to be sad about something that happened to her years ago? And for you to look at your Grandma differently? No! Let's go ride. I want to have a little freedom, so don't tie me too tightly to the other horse because I would like to put my head down and check things out." Her human agreed that the three of them could go for a ride and have some fun.

Yesterday is history. Tomorrow is a mystery. Today is a gift.

Chapter 57: Captain the Horse

When I met Captain, the first thing I noticed about him were his long whiskers.

"Yeah? So what about my long whiskers?" he responded.

I turned to his human and asked her about his whiskers. She said she had learned about the importance of not cutting horses' whiskers and therefore had not trimmed them.

Captain showed me his tail swishing around and around, which his human said he did a lot, especially when he was irritated.

"I am friends with the pheasant," he said, and his human confirmed that there were pheasants in the area.

"I have been on stall rest for the past two months. Boring," Captain added, and his human nodded in agreement.

Captain then showed me a large light in the barn. I didn't quite understand what this meant and asked his human about it. According to his human, the barn gets really dark and that they had watched a movie the weekend before in the barn on the big door. I got chills as she described watching a movie.

"It was a scary movie," he said.

His human laughed and said it was Ghostbusters, but it wasn't a scary movie. Captain said he and the other horses enjoyed it and hoped they would show more films.

I wonder if the makers of Ghostbusters ever envisioned a barn full of horses watching their movie?

Chapter 58: Winky the Saw-whet Owl

I met Winky, a Saw-whet owl who had been brought to a raptor rescue because someone had found him along the side of the road. The rescue team wanted to release the bird back into the wild because he didn't show any signs of injury.

The policy for releasing a bird back out to the wild is that the bird must eat for at least three days and gain weight. But Winky was not eating, and the person in charge was hoping to find out why.

"I don't like what she keeps giving me," Winky said. "She keeps giving me the same stuff. Yuck!"

I turned to the caretaker to ask what she was giving the owl, and she replied that she fed him a normal owl diet of frozen mice.

"She keeps giving me the same mice!" Winky chattered. "I don't like mice. Just because I am an owl doesn't mean I like mice."

"Would he like them better if I cut the tails off before I feed them?" the caretaker wondered.

Winky then began to say some things that really stunned me because they were about me personally: "It's like you and Brussels sprouts. You don't like Brussels sprouts, and if your mom kept feeding you Brussels sprouts you wouldn't eat them. It wouldn't matter if they were cooked in bacon and butter or cheese: they are still Brussels sprouts. You still don't like them, so you would want her to quit feeding them to you."

Winky was completely correct. I am not fond of Brussels sprouts and my mom would try to cook them in different ways to trick me into liking them. But I still hated them! I was flabbergasted as to how this wild creature would know anything about me, my past dislike of Brussels sprouts, and my mother's cooking. Animals have shared a lot of things with me, but this was a first.

The caretaker then asked if Winky would eat a small bird, and the owl said, yes, he would like to have a small bird instead. I told Winky that he needed to eat for three days to gain a little weight and then he would be released back to the wild. He liked this plan and promised to eat the new food.

The next day, I checked up on him to see if he had eaten and I was told he hadn't eaten the small bird. I couldn't believe it, so I asked Winky what they could do to make the bird more palatable.

"She has the bird on its back. I am not going to eat a bird that is on its back. I need to have it look like it is a real bird on its feet," said Winky.

I passed this information along to the caretaker and when she placed the small bird on its belly, the owl ate it! Winky was released back into the wild a week later.

On a side note I would like to add that this type of owl is a very tiny owl. When I did an internet research on the owl I found that the average weight for this type of owl is 80 grams (2.8 ounces). My search also resulted in what type of food these birds eat and included small rodents and birds, which was funny considering that this owl had a specific preference.

This Saw-whet owl may have been little in size, but he was gigantic in personality!

Chapter 59: Lenny the Cat

I chatted with Lenny because his human wanted to know why he disliked the dog so much. When I looked at the picture of Lenny, I immediately felt anger and frustration coming from him. I asked him if he liked the dog.

"No tell them to get rid of the dog," he replied.

Before I told his human what he said, I asked him to tell me the reason he didn't like the dog.

"They never told me they were bringing home a dog. They never even mentioned having a dog. They go out one day and then come home with this piece of shit and they want me to love it. It is a dumb dog. He is dumber than a box of rocks and he is playing on their emotions. Everything was fine before he got here and now the world revolves around him."

I turned to the human and told her what Lenny said, asking if they had talked to the cat beforehand about getting a dog. She shook her head: he was right. One day they came home with a dog with no warning.

"They did not want a dog," Lenny continued. "They went out to see some friends and came home with this dumb dog. Their friends gave them this dog. Now really who gives someone an animal to take care of without asking them about it?"

This all seemed so strange to me so I asked the human to confirm these details. She said they had gone out one day to meet up with friends and the couple gave them a rescue they'd found. Originally, Lenny's humans had no intention of getting a dog, but it all happened so quickly.

Lenny's human felt sorry for the dog and they were hoping the cat would be accepting of it. But he wanted none of it!

"What type of friend gives you an animal you didn't even ask for?" Lenny grumbled. "I don't like that friend either. We were happy before the dog arrived, and now daddy thinks this dumb dog is so great. And look at how much stuff the dog has chewed on! We used to have a nice house and now it's a disaster because of this dumb dog. I do not like the dog, nor do I want the dog to live here."

I had never had an animal tell me something like this with such passion. The cat was quite serious about not wanting the dog to live there.

"She wanted to know how I felt and I am telling her," Lenny added. "The dog needs to find a new home. This is not our problem. It was rude of those people to drop this dog on us."

I then asked Lenny if he had anything else he wanted to share with me, but he said he was done talking to me because he had answered his human's question already. His human promised to tell her husband about Lenny's feelings, and they would have to figure something else out.

"Ask her if she wants the dog. Ask her," Lenny said.

His human was honestly not happy about having the dog either and was still in shock that her friend had given her this dog because she hadn't wanted one. She had been quite happy with Lenny as her only furry family member.

"See she doesn't want the dog either," Lenny said smugly.

I have found that animals are a reflection of their humans, and if *she* didn't like the dog, then no wonder the cat wouldn't like the dog for the same reasons. Great job to Lenny for speaking his mind in such a passionate manner!

Chapter 60: Hootie the Eastern Screech Owl

I first met Hootie and his human several years ago at a senior living facility. When we first chatted, he said: "I am an educational bird. She and I are a team. We are a good team. She educates the people about wildlife, and I get to come out and look at them. We are very good at what we do."

"We had a hell of a ride getting over here," he went on. "She slammed on the brakes and I fell over."

His human said she didn't really remember slamming on the brakes other than to stop for a light, but maybe he thought she had slammed on the brakes.

A year later, I ran into Hootie and his human at another event. The owl wanted me to communicate a couple of things to his human: "Tell her there is a draft. I am cold because there is a draft blowing on me. And tell her I want the music on again. I like music and she isn't playing music. The station needs to be fixed. I like to sing to the music. I don't like talk radio. I like music!"

His human thanked me for letting her know his wishes and promised to do something about the draft and the radio.

A couple of days later, Hootie appeared to me in a dream and asked me to check in with his human to make sure she had fixed the music. When I contacted her, she said she hadn't done it yet but would make a point to check on it that day.

Music was super important to this owl!

Chapter 61: Bailey the Black Lab

I've had the pleasure of chatting with Bailey, one of my friends' furry family member, on several occasions.

Once when I was at a cookout with some friends, I heard Bailey say, "I am not babysitting that puppy." Some friends had brought their brand-new puppy to the cookout and Bailey was not at all interested in it.

Another time I was at a friend's house enjoying the beautiful weather while watching Bailey jump in the pool. I heard the song "I was born this way" by Lady Gaga, and Bailey said: "This is in my bloodline."

I turned to my friend to ask her about what Bailey had said, and she replied that her dog parents were national champion dock dogs so, yes, this was true.

Bailey added: "I can swim better than Michael Phelps."

"How does she know about Michael Phelps?" her human wondered.

"I don't know how animals know about things. But, somehow, she knows about Michael Phelps because she is telling me about him," I replied.

"I am smarter than Einstein!" Bailey declared.

On a third occasion, Bailey's humans had been hanging out at a friend's pool enjoying some adult beverages while Bailey swam and dove for a few hours straight.

"I can't believe she's still swimming!" her human dad commented.

"I can't believe you are still thirsty," Bailey said, speaking of the beverages.

Her humans just started laughing when I told them what she said. I will never look at Michael Phelps without thinking of Bailey!

A few days later, I visited Bailey's humans again and, while we were chatting, Bailey walked over to me, sat down, and said: "Tell her we should be hanging at the neighbors' house. I could swim and you guys could hang out."

When I told my friends what she said, we all just started laughing.

Bailey wasn't laughing; she was serious.

On other occasions, Bailey has told me that her job is to "protect the house," that her favorite foods are fish and hotdogs, and that she loves to play Frisbee.

When they were on vacation, my friend asked me to check in with Bailey to see how she was enjoying their Christmas break in Michigan. "I want to play Frisbee," she told me. They didn't have a Frisbee at the time, but her human bought one and they played together in the snow.

More recently, I chatted with Bailey after the family had gotten back from a trip. She told me to tell her human: "Don't ever give me those pills again." Her human admitted that she had given her some anxiety pills for the twelve-hour car ride.

Whenever I hear the Lady Gaga song "Born This Way," I will always be reminded of Bailey and her passion for swimming.

Chapter 62: Blue the Yellow Lab

I first chatted with Blue when she was here in dog form on earth. Her human wanted to know if she liked a certain type of treat.

"Not the green thing," Blue replied. Her human didn't recall giving her a green treat, but after a few minutes she realized that Blue did not like the treats in the green bag.

Blue showed me a Skunk, but I didn't understand what it meant, so I asked her human about it. The two of them had been out on a walk one day and Blue had gotten sprayed even though her human warned her to stay away from the smelly animal.

"It was a baby and I was trying to help her find her mommy," Blue replied. But her human hadn't found any humor in this because the stench was *terrible*, lingering for days.

Blue then showed me a picture of a cardinal, saying: "The cardinal couldn't fly. I just wanted to play with her. I wasn't going to hurt it." Her human had found a baby cardinal in Blue's mouth and the adult cardinals were attacking her to get their baby back. Her human knew that Blue thought she was only playing, but she had worried about the bird and told Blue to drop it.

Blue wanted the light blankie over her, and her human said she didn't currently put a blanket over her, but would start doing it. She updated me later to say that Blue sighed happily when she covered her with the light blankie.

Blue's energy changed a bit into a stronger more serious tone as she said: "I am *not* fat. I am *not* fat." It felt as if someone had told her she was fat or overweight and she didn't like it. Her human confirmed someone had recently said this about Blue.

"That lady is a bitch! I am not fat. Does she own a full-length mirror?" said Blue.

I didn't know exactly how to say this to Blue's human so I took a couple of deep breaths. "Do you curse?" I asked.

"Yes, why?" Blue's human replied.

"Well, Blue is cursing as she is communicating to me, and I don't want to repeat it unless you curse also."

I told her exactly what Blue told me and she laughed. She told me she could see Blue responding this way to the person who made the remark.

After Blue passed, I connected with her again. One day I was at Blue's human's home and while I was looking at her ashes, I heard her say: "Please tell Grandpa I don't know how to hunt."

"Does your dad hunt?" I asked Blue's human.

Blue's human looked at me like I'd lost my marbles. So, I told her that I was seeing an image of a man in an orange vest.

Her father *had* passed and, when he was here on earth, he had been a pheasant hunter. In life, he'd had a Labrador hunting dog.

Blue's human asked me to pass along a message to Blue: "Tell her it's easy to hunt with Grandpa. Tell her to just pretend the pheasant is a ball and bring it back to him."

I could see Blue smiling at me when her human told me this because I knew Blue loved to play with the ball.

"Grandma rubs my chest till I fall asleep," Blue said.

I asked her human about it and, when she was growing up, her parents had lived with a hunting dog. Her mom had always rubbed its chest until it fell asleep at night. Blue wanted her human to know that Grandma was doing the same thing for her now in the spirit world.

At the end of our conversation Blue told me, "I love being a calendar girl!"

Her human laughed and showed me a calendar she'd made of Blue and their other dog. She'd had the calendar made after Blue passed, so Blue wanted her to know she was happy with it.

Blue said she was with her human's parents in spirit, and they were still doing the things they loved to do while they were here on earth.

I would call Blue's message a very special delivery.

Chapter 63: Akila the Sphynx Cat

Akila means "intelligent", which seemed very appropriate for this cat I communicated with who was *very* smart and opinionated. Her human originally contacted me because she wanted to know if Akila would like a dog or cat sibling.

"No! Hell no," was Akila's immediate response. "I don't mind having the little critters in the house but I do not want a dog or another cat in here. If you want to get a fish, I am okay with it."

Akila said she had known her human in a previous lifetime. According to the cat, she and her human had lived in Egypt during the 14th century and had been best friends. Not everyone believes in past lives (and I must admit that I didn't believe in them either), but I have had animals tell me so many amazing things to open my mind and change my way of thinking.

Akila said she has come back to her human in this life to be her best friend and help her on her journey. The sphynx cat showed me an image of her human healing others, and explained she would be helping. Her human told me she was in the process of learning Reiki healing, and Akila would get right in front of her hands when she was trying to heal people.

The cat just smiled at me.

Akila expressed she enjoyed going outside when the weather was warmer, but did *not* want to wear sunscreen.

"You humans thinking you need to put sunscreen on us cats is crazy. We have lived thousands of years without sunscreen and *now* you think you need to put it on us? I don't want any of that crap put on me. If you feel like you need to put something on me, then get me the sunscreen T-shirt."

Akila showed me a picture of her wearing a white T-shirt made out of sunscreen material. Her human said she would make a note of her request.

This cat's story made me go "Hmm"...sunscreen on cats!?

Chapter 64: Tommy Lee the Turkey

Tommy Lee's human wanted to know if Tommy Lee was happy. When I looked at his picture I immediately felt joy and love.

I was a bit unsure what I was hearing from Tommy Lee when our session started. I thought I heard him say, "I have a cute waddle. I have a cute wobble." I wasn't quite sure what he meant by waddle or wobble, thinking he might be referring to the way he walked. I told his human the exact words I heard and asked if he had a cute walk.

She laughed and remarked, "I understand what he means. I tell him all the time he has a cute wattle. It's the flap of skin hanging off his chin."

I laughed because I thought he was talking about his strut, and he was talking about a body part instead.

I saw an image of red food that looked like cranberries to me and Tommy Lee smiling. His human had given him cranberries and strawberries and he seemed to enjoy the strawberries more.

"Yuck grapes," Tommy Lee added.

"Yeah, I threw him some grapes as well," his human chuckled, "but he didn't like them."

"I am like a dog. I am like a dog," said Tommy Lee. His human seemed to think him quite dog-like as he often followed her around the farm.

"She has my nose art. She has my nose art," Tommy Lee said twice.

His human had seen his nose-prints on the window because he liked to look in the porch window to see what was happening inside the house.

I asked Tommy Lee if he was happy, and he said: "I am not as sad as she thinks I am. I want to spend more time with her. I love her and want to spend more time with her." His human shared with me that things at work had gotten really busy and she wasn't able to spend the time outside like she had during the summer.

"Tell her to meditate outside and put it on a speaker so I can hear, too," he said. "Tell her not to use the earbuds. I want to be able to hear the meditation."

"Wow!" his human responded. "I have been trying to get back into meditation but haven't been very successful, and I do wear earbuds when I do it."

"I don't live in a chicken coop. I live in a shed," said Tommy Lee. His human said he did sleep in a shed at night but had freedom during the day.

Tommy Lee explained: "I have a window in my shed. I have a 'She-Shed. Cheryl's She-Shed.'"

The turkey had me laughing at his comment about Cheryl's She-Shed!

"Yes, he has a window in the shed so he can see outside, but it isn't a fancy shed," said his human with a smile.

Tommy Lee did a fabulous job throwing his humor into our conversation. Whenever I see the State Farm Insurance commercial with "Cheryl's She-Shed", I am reminded of Tommy Lee the turkey.

Chapter 65: Betty the Chicken

Betty's human asked me to come chat with her horse in person, but as soon as I got my car door closed I began to hear Betty: "Who are you? Are you the animal communicator? Are you here to talk to the horse? She's is a hot mess you know. It's my job to know what is going on at the farm. If you are an animal communicator, why aren't you responding to me?"

Betty continued to chatter away as her human and I were walking up to the barn. I asked if we could pause for a minute because her chicken insisted on speaking first. When we stopped, I looked at Betty and she tilted her head.

I began to answer her questions out loud: "Yes, I am an animal communicator. Yes, I am here to talk the horse and, yes, I can see how you know everything going on at the farm. The reason I didn't respond sooner was because you were talking so fast I didn't have time to respond."

Betty yelled loudly: "Hey everyone, the animal communicator is here and she can really hear us."

I told Betty that, if there was something she wanted to share with her human, I would be happy to pass on the message.

"I am a special chicken. I am a very special bird," Betty said.

Her human confirmed Betty was indeed a special bird because she was her daughter's 4H project.

"I am a very special chicken," the chicken repeated.

"I think she is referring to her breed when she tells you she is special. She is a rare Orpington chicken," said her human, which immediately gave me goosebumps.

"Sweet," said Betty, who then showed me a glass of iced tea. Her human chuckled, sharing with me that the two of them sometimes sat out on the porch, and Betty liked to put her head in her glass of tea. Her human thought Betty liked the sweet tea more than the unsweetened kind.

"Tell her the neighbor across the way is very nosey. She watches what goes on over here through her windows. She is very nosey. She is like Gladys Kravitz," Betty added.

"Betty is right! Our neighbor is very nosey, but she is a nice lady, so I don't mind," her human replied. "You know, I think it is ironic that Betty is saying our neighbor is like Gladys Kravitz. My husband and I compare Betty to Gladys Kravitz because she has to know what everyone is doing on the farm. Talk about the pot calling the kettle black!"

"I protect the farm and am really good at it," said Betty. Her human confirmed she was good at protecting the farm because she always makes lots of noise when there was something happening.

"Tell her I love my human and want to spend more time with her," the chicken requested. Her human promised to encourage her daughter to come out and spend more time with her.

Betty looked at me and said: "Alright I am done with you. I wanted to see if you were the real deal and you are. You can now go talk to that crazy horse. She needs help. Thank you for talking to me, and I hope you have a good day."

Betty the chicken might have been small in size, but she was big in personality!

Chapter 66: Penelope the Schnauzer

Penelope was newly adopted and her new human reached out to me to have a conversation with her to see how she liked her new home. I had such a good time communicating with Penelope that by the time I was done having our session, my stomach ached from laughing!

"I am a princess. I am a princess. I am a princess," Penelope said not once but *three* times to make sure I heard her properly. Her humans were just saying the night before our session that they thought she was turning into a princess. Well she wanted to let them know that, yes, she was indeed a princess.

"What is her favorite place to sleep?" her human asked.

Penelope showed me a picture of her sleeping on a pillow right by her human's head. I thought it was funny because normally I see cats sleeping by their humans' heads, but not a dog. Her human confirmed this to be true.

Penelope kept showing me a picture of the pillow, and I felt like there was something very special about it. I asked her human if it was a feather pillow or a memory foam pillow. Her human shook her head no, but Penelope continued to show me the pillow and I kept getting the feeling that it was somehow very special.

After a minute, her human said, "I think I know what she may be trying to tell you. The pillow she likes is the My Pillow brand." I immediately got the chills!

Penelope was trying to tell me that her human does lay her head on a "very special pillow." Her human laughed and promised to purchase one for her.

Next, Penelope showed me her favorite place to sit and look out the window, which she called her "princess" chair. Her human said the dog did indeed have a special chair.

Then Penelope said she did *not* like having her nails messed with and showed me a picture of a bowl of vanilla ice cream. She liked ice cream and wanted to lick the bowl more often.

Before our session ended, Penelope communicated that she would like to have a new "princess" collar. She asked for a pink collar with rhinestones. Her human said they had just talked about getting her a new collar, but they didn't want anything with rhinestones on it. Well, Penelope was letting them know that she knew about the conversation and wanted the rhinestones!

A few days after the session, Penelope's human sent me an email with an update from our session:

> *We* did *get a new collar for Penelope! Pink with diamonds and pearls! LOL! I am sending you a picture of her wearing it while taking watch on her 'princess chair.' She has been such a hoot! I swear she has come out of her shell more.*
>
> *I told my teenagers all about our session! One of them was so excited to hear about it and has been gathering new questions for another session in the near future.*

My other teenager first told me that he's not really a believer, but still wanted to hear what Penelope had to say. Well, once I gave him some details he has changed his mind, especially when I was telling him about Penelope not liking her nails to be messed with. Initially, I honestly thought, 'What dog doesn't like their nails messed with when at the groomer or getting trimmed?' Well, come to find out, my one teenager would mess with her nails at home. He started smirking!

We have all been reminding Penelope that this is her forever home and that she belongs here. We also let her have a little lick of the bowl with vanilla ice cream as well! Oh yes, I gave her my My Pillow since we have extras that we keep out for guests.

I wonder if the My Pillow company has ever thought about making dog beds. Maybe Penelope could be their spokes-dog!

Chapter 67: Louie XIV the Papillon

W hen we had our first session, Louie was living in a foster home, so I informed him that he would be leaving his foster home to go to his soon-to-be permanent home. His human wanted to have a session with him before he arrived to make sure he was okay with relocating.

I started off by asking Louie if he was happy with the upcoming relocation, and he replied: "I am *thrilled* to be going to my new home!"

Louie's bag was packed and he already knew about the brown and black blankie and the new stuffed toy his female human had bought him. He also knew his human daddy wasn't thrilled about the adoption, but didn't seem to be worried because he would have him "wrapped around his paw within the month." He showed me a man driving around in a truck with Louie inside and said the two of them would be riding around together often.

A couple of days before the official adoption day, I awoke to a vision of Louie jumping up and down smiling and singing "On the road again, I can't wait to get on the road again!" He had my full attention, so I asked him what he wanted me to know because I could feel his extremely joyous energy. He communicated to me that he would see his new humans at 10am on Saturday and that he was so thrilled to be going home.

Later that morning, I called Louie's soon-to-be new human and told her the message he had told me. She could not confirm this day or time because it was a long drive to the foster home and they hadn't scheduled an official time with the rescue staff.

A few days after Louie arrived at his new home, I got an email from his human saying they had driven over *eight* hours to pick him up. When she had called to set up the appointment to pick him up from the foster home, they gave her a time of 10am despite not knowing what Louie had told me. I find it truly amazing that Louie knew what time they were meeting and had been able to communicate it to me!

Louie was right about so many things he couldn't have known, like the blankie and stuffed toy his human had bought for the car ride home. In our session, he had promised to give his human a big kiss when he first met her, and Louie's human said he had done just as he said he would.

The dog said, "I am royalty and I would like to have a royal name." When they arrived home, his humans gave him a new name: Louie XIV.

I got an update from Louie's human shortly after he had settled in to his new home. He'd only been with them for five days but acted as if he were at home and got along well with his new dog sibling.

Louie had plans to "wrap daddy around his paw," and his female human could see that Louie was indeed working hard on building a relationship with his male human. She told me Louie follows him all around the house and daddy has given him a nickname: Fourteen.

I believe Louie succeeded in building a strong bond with both of his humans and is living life to the fullest in his forever home.

Chapter 68: From the Human's Point of View

I have decided to include a few sessions from the human's point of view so you could get a feel for how humans reacted to what they learn in my sessions. Here are a few follow-up responses from amazed clients:

A rat terrier named Zeb from his human's view:

I met Zeb at the AKC Nationals dog show in Orlando, Florida. These are her direct words:

You told me he said he was "done" with conformation, so I asked you what he would be interested in. I suggested Barnhunt, at which time he confirmed vigorously. I promised him Barnhunt when he earned his conformation Grand Championship. We competed in barnhunt for the first time last week. In addition to his five first places he also got high in class on 4 of those 5 runs! (He missed a complete sweep by 1 second!) He told you he would win more ribbons than he already had in conformation, and he did.

Zeb and I thank you! No more conformation for Zeb, lots of rats though.

Written by Anna M.

A golden retriever named Nash from his human's view:

N ash's story is an example of a dog being his own health advocate. Nash repeatedly told his humans he was not going to die, which gave them hope and the drive to push for answers.

We met Cindy in early 2018 and after several phone conversations we decided to take both of our dogs [Hallie and Nash] to visit her. We found out a lot of things we wondered about and got Nash's thoughts on getting a sister golden, which he wasn't excited about. We think he is selfish and wants us to himself! We found out he likes to work and really likes obedience training.

In late June, Nash started coughing occasionally. After a short period of time it began to get more regular and seemed to get deeper. We took him to the vet several times, but the vet was unable to come up with a reason for it. The x-ray and blood work wasn't showing anything, but the cough persisted. The vet was at a loss, and we started thinking that maybe it was some type of infection. By this time, we could tell Nash wasn't feeling well. He stopped wanting to play and only wanted to sleep.

The weekend before his next appointment, worry started to set in because he was getting pretty weak. We live about 45 minutes from Cindy, and Donna asked if she would talk to Nash. She said of course she would, so Donna took Nash up to see Cindy.

When she arrived, she asked: "What brings you here today?"

And Donna replied, "His health."

Donna explained that we had been to the vet three times, and we were getting ready to go again but were wondering if you [Cindy] were picking up on anything. At no point did we say anything that was going on or any of the treatments. While they were talking, Cindy mentioned that she felt pain in her chest, meaning she was picking this up from Nash. He felt pain in his chest or abdomen.

She mentioned more than once him saying "I'm not dying" or "I'm not gonna' die. They just haven't found it yet." Cindy told Donna to tell the vet to check his chest again.

On Monday morning, Craig took Nash to the vet and had more x-rays taken. Still, nothing was showing up. The vet started palpating his abdomen and next thing she says was "This isn't right."

I asked what wasn't right, and she said, "This lump in his lower abdomen."

We took another x-ray, and sure enough it showed a mass about the size of my fist. I asked the vet what would happen next. She recommended an ultrasound to get a better look.

A couple of days later, we had an ultrasound and it showed a definite mass in his abdomen, but they could not tell if it was attached. The next thing out of Craig's mouth was "What are our options?"

The vet said, "Well, we can leave it, or we can take it out."

"Get it out!" Craig said.

The vet could schedule the surgery for the following Tuesday. Craig replied, "I don't want it there. It's not supposed to be there. Get it out!"

The vet stepped out of the room and then returned about five minutes later and said, "I spoke with the surgeon, and he agreed to do the surgery tonight."

The next nine hours were nerve racking for both of us, not knowing what was going on. Around 9:15 pm, we got a phone call saying the surgery had been a success. She followed up the phone call with a couple pictures of him in the kennel recovering. She said it was a large mass and said she would send it in to find out what it was.

Fast forward a week and we got the results: spindle cell sarcoma. Cancer. But they were very positive they had gotten all of it.

So here we are, 6 months later, and Nash is doing fine. Cindy spoke to Nash over the phone awhile back and he said, "I'm a miracle!"

Yes, he is! He is our miracle boy! Many thanks to God, the vet team, and another close friend who is a vet, and most certainly our breeder. They are the reason we kept our sanity and have a happy nine-year-old Golden Retriever.

As I sit here tonight in the recliner, Nash is laying right beside me beside my legs. My guess is he knows I am writing about him.

Written by Craig S.

A cat named Toby from his human's view:

When I met with Toby I had no idea he was going to be so humorous. It was a pleasure communicating with him while he was here on earth and again after he crossed the rainbow bridge.

When you first walked in the door at my house, my orange tabby cat named Toby was lying in the sun by the sliding glass door. He said: "I suppose you're here to talk to me. I don't need therapy, but my sisters do."

Then he proceeded to say, "My mommy has got a heart of gold, but she worries too much. She needs to go outside, walk around in the garden barefoot, and lie down in the grass to enjoy the sunlight."

He said he loves the sunlight and warmth, especially when he gets to lie in mommy's big leather chair. He said, "I'm not going to live forever, but let's enjoy every day while I'm here." (Toby was diagnosed with diabetes, pancreatitis, and irritable bowel syndrome).

Toby also said he liked room temperature water but didn't like cold water. He wanted to know if mommy would leave the TV on when she goes to work because it's too quiet in the house. He talked about being punished and locked in the bathroom for something his sister had done and said of this experience "that sucked."

He wanted to know if mommy would play with the feathers and toys and the laser light more because he really enjoyed it. He also loved the big rock in the backyard; it made him feel safe and was always warm. Toby said the neighbor's dog who barked all the time was annoying and asked if I could do anything about it. He said there was a cricket in the basement who sang all night long and asked to see it when mommy finds it.

Then he told you it was time for you to go now he had nothing more to say.

Several months later Toby told us he started to have a lot of stomach aches and it was time for him to go because "he had golden wings waiting for him." He wanted to go with his dignity instead of throwing up on the floor and missing the litter box. (He said he would still torment his little sister.)

Toby promised to send me gold butterflies after he crossed the rainbow bridge to let me know he was okay. And the next week after he passed I had hundreds of gold butterflies on my flowers in the garden. Toby now has his golden wings and thanks mommy for them.

Cindy Downing

Written by Karen H.

A dog named Issebelle
from her human's view:

When I connected with Issebelle I immediately could feel the love for her human and her humor. I am grateful to her human for sharing her story.

I had Issebelle for almost twelve years. Oh my gosh, she was my best friend! I am a massage therapist and when my clients would come in, she would always greet them at the door, lie in her bed during their massage, and then walk them out. Perfect little lady and healer!

Well, then Issebelle started having trouble with her kidneys and this health problem forced her to move on. I was literally sick. There were times I could not even breathe it was so terrible. I would tell myself it was crazy to be this way, but the loss was so great!

Fortunately, one day a client of mine said she had a friend who communicated with animals who have crossed over. Oh boy, I could not wait to talk with this lady!

I then meet with Cindy brought a picture of Issebelle and my five questions. It was amazing! Cindy started doing her thing, and the next thing I knew she was talking to my Issebelle. I was so very excited!

Cindy told me many things about Issebelle. There was no way Cindy could have known these things, but she was right on, right to her favorite tree in the back yard (an evergreen tree). I would look out my kitchen window and all I would see was her little black butt. She was for sure sniffing out a bunny.

Issebelle also told Cindy she was a greeter on the rainbow bridge, and that they even gave her some wings that were small and black, just like her. How beautiful! And all of this made sense because she was also a greeter here on earth. After hearing many wonderful things, I told Issebelle I felt she'd gone too soon and that our work together was not done. She told Cindy, "Well it is very rare, but I will be coming back!" It would be over a year, and she did not want me to look for her. Talk about being excited!

A little over a year later, I felt this need to get ahold of Cindy and I did. We got together and she confirmed it was time to start looking for Issebelle.

Cindy said I would find Issebelle through the internet. She said she was also doing "charity work" on the other side, and when she comes back she wants a royal name. The puppy would have a cute little hop and a heart somewhere on her.

Then I asked, "But how will I know it is really you?" and Cindy said to remember the feeling of when I found her.

I went home and sat on my computer all night! All I could find were puppies for $1,300 that I couldn't afford. Before I went to bed, I said, "Lord, if I am to have this puppy, I need your help."

Much to my surprise, the next morning I started up my iPad and the very first page was a site with puppies. As I looked down the row, there she was: a puppy named Angel Eyes. This was her!

I called the lady and she was still for sale. Of course, I had a full day with clients, but the lady promised to hold her for me. I could not get there fast enough and when I held her, I knew. The first thing she did was lay her head on my heart just as Issebelle had done when she had moved on. I knew instantly it was my Issebelle.

There were three things that also confirmed this: the lady's name Charity, the dog had a cute little hop, and she had a toy in the shape of a heart in the bag that was coming home with me.

I am very blessed to have Issebelle's spirit back and renamed her Princess Lilly Rose. It is hard to explain that she is a new dog, not just like Issebelle, but her spirit is definitely here with me. I am so blessed to have had this experience with Cindy!

Written by Arlene D.

A dog named Max from his human's view:

Max communicated several different signs he was going to send his human, and she was able to validate them as you will see in the following story.

The session I had with Cindy for my dog, Max, was one of the most fulfilling and happy times for me. I really missed him tremendously and just needed to hear from him.

The first thing he said was that he was not my first choice, which sounds worse than it was. But he was a gift to me and my husband on Christmas Eve. It was a total surprise and shock to me, and I wasn't really prepared to have a dog. He was going to get bigger than any dog I wanted if I did have a dog, so there was a lot of conflict and decision-making. But he won my heart and was the best gift I have ever gotten.

He went everywhere with me, and Cindy picked up on this as well. She said he was my copilot which he truly was because he always rode with me on the front seat and looked like a human person sitting there.

She felt he was somewhat of a therapy dog and he certainly was. He never went through the training for it, but he visited my brother's care facility for years and made everyone there happy just by his presence and demeanor.

When I asked Cindy how I would know if Max was around me, she told me he was going to send me orange butterflies, specifically monarchs. This really hit home because, just prior to my reading, I had gotten two milkweed plants to help our neighborhood bring the monarch butterflies back to our area. She also said he would bring me yellow birds.

I feed squirrels and birds in my backyard every day. I love to look for yellow finches but never see them. I couldn't remember the last time I actually saw one in my yard. Anyhow, later that afternoon when I got home, I was in my kitchen and happened to glance out my window to my birdfeeders and, lo and behold, there was a yellow finch on the lower peg of the feeder and then a second one landed on the top of the hanger. I couldn't believe it! I took pictures. I was thrilled to say the least!

A few hours later, I went over to a nearby shop to buy some sandwiches for supper and parked my car. The car directly in front of me had an Iowa license plate, which had on it a yellow finch sitting on a pink flower. I was shocked! Iowa license plates don't look like that normally. It was definitely one of those specially made ones, but I have never seen one like it before. So I took a picture of that as well.

Later, I downloaded the pictures I had taken of the symbols Max had sent me and noticed on the license plate right beside the bird and flower was the name "Al," which is my father's name. He had passed away as well. That was amazing! In addition to that incredible coincidence (and I no longer believe things are just coincidence), I remembered that in my office, where Max's kennel was and where we spent a lot of time together, on the wall hangs a beautiful painting by P. Buckley Moss of two yellow finches on the same pink flower. She had been commissioned by Iowa to paint that picture as a fundraiser for the state, and I had bought one. It must be their state bird and flower. Max and I must have looked at that picture every day for years.

The next day when I needed a sympathy card for someone, I decided to go through the stack of the ones we get in the mail from different charities. As I went through them, I came across two birthday cards depicting two, big, beautiful yellow finches with the monarch butterfly up in the corner.

I was blown away. Another sign from my dear Max. I now have one card in my office and one somewhere else where I would see them at all times.

A few weeks later, I ran into Cindy again and told her I hadn't heard anything from Max in a while. She said, "Mother's

Day is just a couple of days away, and I have a feeling you'll see another one then."

Sure enough, I did. It sat for a brief time near my bird feeder, and then one flew over and sat on my neighbor's feeder for quite some time while I was watching it. Of course, I took a picture. Just the other day, I actually saw another one at my feeder.

Later on, when I was driving, the pickup truck in front of me had the license plate that said, "Papa x 2." To me, this meant my dad, who we called Papa, times his only two great-grandchildren. I noticed at the very bottom, kind of hidden by the license plate cover, that right below "Papa x 2" it said, "My dog is my copilot." So, I got another license plate with a message from my dad and from my precious dog. I can't tell you how much these messages mean to me.

Cindy had asked me if I wanted to ask Max anything, so I asked where he liked to sleep best. She asked if I had a light-colored comforter on my bed and I said, yes, I did. She said he always slept down towards the foot end of my bed and visits me there. She said he doesn't sleep by the pillow, which he never did, but would often jump off because he was too hot.

This made me start thinking of something that had been happening for a long time and never understood. When I would roll over at night, I would sometimes hear this thud like something was falling off my bed and I never could figure out what it was. There just was absolutely nothing on my bed that could've rolled off and nothing that would've made a sound. It finally dawned on me: it was probably Max jumping off the bed. So now I just say "Hi" to him and ask him to come back whenever I hear it.

Another stunning thing Cindy told me was that she kept seeing tufts of hair. Whenever I would brush Max, I would save his hair. I'd heard of people weaving dog hair into scarves or hats and had thought I might use the saved hair someday. Most of it is in a bag, but I did save one tuft of his hair and put it on my bedroom dresser so I would be able to touch and feel it after he died. It was pretty remarkable that she picked up on this.

She mentioned I had recently moved his collar, which I had. He's been gone for almost two years, but I had not really put away his collar. It remained in the place it always had when he was alive, and I had just recently moved it to rest with some of his other belongings.

Cindy also knew he'd had a bad eye, but she said it wasn't as bad as I thought. I had thought it was bad enough to have eye surgery, but he thought that the worst part was the stupid cone, of course. But it really did make his vision better.

She said he was a gift, which was true. He would bring me botanical things, especially when he was a puppy. Every time he went out he would bring me a leaf or a pinecone back. It was really sweet.

She explained that he wasn't in pain, it was fine with him that I'd had to put him to sleep, and he had met St. Francis when he crossed the rainbow bridge. It was one of the hardest decisions I'd ever had to make, but he let me know he did not suffer and it was his time to go.

I miss him so much and would really love the companionship of another dog, but I just don't know if I could right now. Cindy informed me that he would come back again as a small dog because he doesn't want me to miss joy and laughter in my life. I thought she meant the new puppy my son just got, which I will pet-sit a lot because they work so much. But she said, no, it would be my own dog and it would happen in six to eight months from now. It will be something I would not go out and seek or buy; it would just happen somehow. If I decided to accept this dog, it would be Max and I would know him by staring into his eyes. (We used to stare into each other's eyes a lot. Time will tell!) She went on to say that he doesn't want to be called "Max" in his new life, and he will not be the same breed of dog. He will be a small, white, fluffy dog.

I asked him if he knew of a little animal I had befriended since he had departed this world. I didn't say what kind it was.

He kept telling Cindy it wasn't a real animal. I kept saying, "Yes, it is."

When I finally told her it was a squirrel, she said, "Well, he doesn't think it's a real animal."

Pretty funny, but the squirrels really do mean a lot to me because they take peanuts out of my hand, and it's at least something to love when I don't have my Max.

All in all, this session with Cindy was one of the best things I've ever done for myself. I can't thank her enough. She has such a wonderful gift, and I treasure all the things she has shared with me.

Written by Sandy K.

Chapter 69: That's A Wrap!

I want to take a moment to say a huge "Thank you!" to you, the reader, for spending your hard-earned money to purchase this book and for opening your mind up to the possibility of animals being able to communicate with humans. I hope this book has gotten you to look at things from a different perspective.

Please remember, animals...

1. are full of life with their own unique personalities.
2. need certainty and validation that they are in their "forever home."
3. are highly opinionated and intelligent.
4. are joyful creatures full of humor, jokes, and silliness just like humans.
5. are sensitive to their human's behavior, thoughts, and feelings that they sometimes mirror them.
6. know many things that we humans don't.

I cannot stress this enough: animals do not want to have humans focus on the days they were sick or their final days of life. They want us to remember the fun times, the silly times, the things that make humans laugh and smile. Animals have repeatedly told me to tell their humans they do not want them to have guilt with regards to having to make the decision to release them to the other side. Numerous animals have told me when they cross the rainbow bridge it is like a birthday to them because they have a new form and are in perfect health once again.

When your animals cross over into the spirit world, please remember that they are still very much a part of your life. Animals love to send signs to their humans to let them know they are still around. I always tell people to be open minded to the different ways you can receive a sign. For example, a rainbow doesn't have to be a real rainbow in the sky. The rainbow can be in the form of a sticker, on a card, in a storefront window or on someone's T-shirt.

I end this book with something I continuously say to people: Animals are AMAZING!

Acknowledgements

M ost importantly, I want to say thank you to all the animals here on earth and in spirit form who encouraged me to share their stories. Without them this book would not have come together. It was at their urging and persistence (and, believe me, they are very persistent) that I write this book to show the world animal communication is real.

To my husband, Bruce, I want to say thank you from the bottom of my heart for supporting me through this adventure. You have been my partner, bodyguard, consultant, promoter, driver, and biggest cheerleader. I can't tell you how much I appreciate all you have done and continue to do for me. I know it isn't easy living with someone who talks to animals, so thank you for being patient and understanding.

To my sister, Teresa, thank you for always taking time to listen to me talk about animal communication. I know sometimes you think I am crazy, but you don't show it. I am so thankful you are my sister and love you dearly.

To my friend, Gina, I want to thank you for your expertise on the design of my book cover. You are extremely talented and I appreciate you sharing your gift with me. I thank you for all the years of friendship and for your advice. Your words of wisdom are absolutely priceless.

To Dr. Michelle, I can't say thank you enough for taking such wonderful care of our beloved dog, Rosie. I am grateful to call you my friend.

To Chelsey, thank you for assistance with our furry family members and for listening to their words of wisdom as you worked with them. I know it hasn't been easy when you have me telling you exactly what they are saying.

To my friends the "Light Ladies" I am forever grateful for our gatherings and friendship. You all are very special lightworkers, keep shining your bright light in the world.

And, finally, to my furry family members, Darcy, Winston, and Rosie (in spirit) I appreciate all your help and advice with regards to my sessions and while I have been writing this book. The three of you continue to bring joy to my life!